Longing *to* Know

Longing *to* Know

Esther Lightcap Meek

Brazos Press

A Division of Baker Book House Co
Grand Rapids, Michigan 49516

Published by Brazos Press
a division of Baker Publishing Group
P.O. Box 6287, Grand Rapids, MI 49516-6287
www.brazospress.com

Library of Congress Cataloging-in-Publication Data
Meek, Esther L. 1953-
    Longing to know / Esther Lightcap Meek.
        p.   cm.   ·
    Includes bibliographical references.
    ISBN 10: 1-58743-060-6 (pbk.)
    ISBN 978-1-58743-060-2 (pbk.)
        1. Knowledge, Theory of (Religion) 2. Christianity—Philosophy. I. Title.
BT50.M44 2003
231'.042—dc21   2003000142

Contents

Foreword

This is a book about knowing. Knowing is an activity that all of us are involved in, all of the time. Usually knowing happens without our taking great thought to the process. But sometimes we stop and think about what we're doing. When we stop and think, what we were doing without much thought becomes murky indeed.

It's good and useful to stop and think about knowing, even if it means tackling something murky. For one thing, the circumstances of our lives at times force us into the cellar, so to speak, to examine the foundations of our beliefs. For another, the exercise serves to enhance and extend our everyday knowing, as well as give us fresh confidence in our efforts.

▉ Who Needs to Read This Book, and Why

This book is written for all knowers. But it in particular targets knowers propelled into the cellar of their beliefs by one or more of the following circumstances of life.

First, I have in mind people who wrestle with questions concerning truth and the possibility of knowledge as a result our culture's recent consensus shift from modernism to postmodernism. Philosophically, the shift has been centuries in the making, but it has only in recent decades reached the street. We have gone from struggling to conform to stringent criteria to shore up our claims to absolute, objective truth to outright rejection of the entire enterprise—from absolute truth to no truth. Affirming no truth is not always a comfortable position for a human being. It leaves nagging questions. This book deals with those questions.

A second huge "circumstance" of life is growing up—moving from adolescence to adulthood. This changeover, in our day and age, quite frankly takes a long time. People who are middle aged like me can feel as if they are still growing up. I have first-hand experience! At the other end of the age spectrum, we often comment, young people are forced to grow up sooner than they used to. Your particular age doesn't qualify you for or disqualify you from this category. What qualifies you is that you deal with questions about what is really real and good and how you know, questions to which you were presuming someone else's answers but now are faced with deciding for yourself. As we grow up, we often have to take that trip to the cellar to scrutinize the foundations of our beliefs. This book aids that foray.

Third, this book is written for people who are considering questions about truth and how we know because they are considering Christianity. Christianity is the belief that what the Holy Bible says about God and his relationship to the world is true, and that trusting Jesus is the only way to be right with God. It involves, in short, affirming that certain claims are *true*. People considering Christianity includes people who have not yet embraced it, as well as people who have, but want or need to think it through more deeply.

Affirming the claims of Christianity has always involved people in thinking about why those claims are not *wrong*. This is how things were when I was a child. Later, affirming Christianity involved people in defending why those claims were not *meaningless*. I felt this in my late teens and early twenties, as I encountered philosophies that argued that only sense perception–based scientific claims were meaningful, and the rest—religious, psychological, ethical, artistic, and historical—were more like gibberish. But in the postmodern era, affirming Christian claims as true involves people in defending, often in the face of tremendous wrath, why those claims are not *morally outrageous*. A claim that something is universally true is something akin to Hitler's concentration camps, a huge and damaging imposition on others' freedom. People considering Christianity, then, simply cannot avoid the more foundational questions concerning truth. To these people, I very much want this book to bring direction and hope.

8

▉ My Debt to Michael Polanyi, and Others

In these pages I develop a proposal concerning how knowing works. I believe that many questions can be answered at least preliminarily, and many puzzles solved, and personal hope of truth restored, by appropriating this model of how we know. I believe the model is confirmed by the ordinary day-to-day experiences of every human being.

The model of knowing I use belongs first to scientist and philosopher Michael Polanyi. A Hungarian who died in 1976, Polanyi published books and essays from the 1940s to the 1960s that at the time were not widely known or received. His message was revolutionary and consequently inflammatory. Recent shifts in philosophical outlook, I believe, have had the result that more people are taking notice of what he had to say.

I have chosen not to say, "Polanyi says . . ." at every turn in this book, although I could have! I have done this, first of all, because I want this book not to read like a textbook, but rather like a personal meditation.

Second, I have thought about Polanyi's model for at least twenty years. For my doctorate I wrote a dissertation on his work. Recently I have looked back and recognized a gradual movement in my life from describing his work to taking it as a personal working hypothesis in thinking about knowing, to downright appropriating it. I commend it to you now as very much my own conviction. You will see that it shapes my understanding of many aspects of my life. In fact, I try to live his model, and I try to help the reader do that too. I have applied it in fresh ways. Polanyi never knew popular postmodernism. I believe that his model nevertheless contains within in it a profound response. Polanyi's model was not developed primarily to accommodate theism; it is my claim that it aptly suits what Scripture indicates about human knowing. Polanyi's environment, as a scientist, was the research lab; mine, as a teacher and mom, has been, so to speak, the kitchen table (that wonderful place where teaching and parenting intersect!).

And third, in the process of appropriating Polanyi, I have also adapted the model, especially in light of the contributions of theologian John Frame, whose work I take to represent accurately the stipulations about human knowing indicated by Scripture. One very helpful feature of Frame's approach is his consistent delineation of three dimensions of human knowing. In this book I refer to them as the world, the self, and the word, or directions. I unpack Polanyi's model in reference to these three dimensions.

So please do not take my avoiding reference to his name as discredit to Polanyi! If you want to get the model from the horse's mouth, in its pristine and authoritative statement, read his works. See especially his *Personal Knowledge: Towards a Post-Critical Philosophy* (Chicago: University of Chicago Press, 1958) and *The Tacit Dimension* (Garden City, N.Y.: Doubleday Anchor Books, 1966).

The application of this model to knowing auto mechanics and God, with critical reliance on the Holy Bible and the compelling insights additionally of John Calvin, C. S. Lewis, Lesslie Newbigin, Annie Dillard, and numerous others, is my own personal, risky, and responsible submission in pursuit of reality.

My auto mechanic, featured in this book's "driving" illustration, merits my gratitude. I am grateful for his reliable character, skill, and service. I include in my gratitude not only Jeff, but his entire staff at the Kirkwood Citgo. Not many people enjoy such confidence in their auto mechanics. But Jeff has no idea how he will serve to expedite many people's understanding of knowing, and knowing God. This, as a surprising manifestation of unanticipated consequences, is indeed a confirmation of his reality.

My children, Starr, Stacey, and Stephanie, have also proven fruitful sources of illustrations. They have made me both a mom and a philosopher, and have dwelt graciously with the blend.

I dedicate this book to my first philosophy teacher, mentor, and inspiration for my pursuits, Jim Grier, most recently dean at Grand Rapids Baptist Seminary. I switched colleges and majors to study with him on the strength of a description given by one of his students. I sensed the possibility of indeterminate future manifestations, and the risky choice has shaped everything wonderful about my life since then.

I dedicate it, second, to my colleague and friend-of-my-mind, theologian Mike Williams, with whom I teach epistemology at Covenant Seminary, and whose theological and philosophical insights regularly engage me and prompt me to worship God.

This book is dedicated, third, to the stellar students of Epistemology 2000. Adding hours of enthusiastic after-class discussion to the requisite class time, they bought into my vision, and responded to my efforts with encouragement and love. This is the book they asked for. In particular, Michael Gordon and Jon Dunning have loyally cheered me on. Michael's story I describe in these pages.

■ Tips for Reading This Book

Finally, I want to advise you concerning how to read this book. Philosophical questions, questions about how we know and what is really real, are inher-

10

ently difficult questions. I have wanted very much in this book to deal with them in a popular and accessible way. I have often wondered if this goal was oxymoronic, inherently contradictory! But I profoundly believe that it is or must be possible, because I believe that every human being, not just the philosophy majors, wrestles with the BHQs, as I call them—the Big Hairy Questions of what is true, what is good, and what is real. Thus, philosophy should be written in a way that will help everybody.

But you very likely will find this book dense at places, and you may feel often that you do not entirely grasp what is being said. Please hear my encouragement: the problem isn't you. And I hope—I have striven to make it so that— the problem isn't entirely me. The problem is the enterprise itself. Philosophy is difficult. The questions are "hairy." Philosophy is difficult, like looking directly at the tip of your nose is difficult! We rely in every act of knowing on foundational philosophical beliefs. It takes an effort to put into words the convictions we know usually only in our relying on them. It takes a huge effort to put into words what lies at the border of, and perhaps beyond, articulation. But please press on—even gaining partial understanding is an act of personal integrity and very much worth the effort.

To compensate for the density of the subject, you may find it helps to follow this advice. First, read one chapter per sitting. I have purposely made each chapter short. We are busy people. I can conceive of you reading one chapter a week, then thinking about it as you drive to work or school, cook, shower, garden, or watch your baby play. I hope you might be able to discuss it with a soul mate. You may want to refer to the chapter throughout your ruminations. You can use the questions at the end of each chapter to direct your thought and personal application.

Second, read "through your eyelashes." By this I mean, don't strive necessarily to understand every word precisely. You can get the gist or the feel of the thing even if you don't get every single word. Be patient, for your grasp, I promise, will grow as you continue to read through the chapters. You will see that this advice grows consistently out of my convictions concerning how coming to know happens. I have tried to write the book in a way that matches these convictions. I have only words at my disposal. So I have wanted to use the words not only to represent but also to evoke your felt sense of your own knowing.

Third, try to apply what you read to your own experience. I have in writing this book told numerous stories and offered many examples from my own life. Please match my stories with your own. My heartfelt longing for this book is that it will lend significance to your own longing for reality and for truth, that it will guide your search, and that it will give you hope.

■ For Further Thought and Discussion

Get a journal. At the end of each chapter in this book, you will find questions and activities that you can use to prompt your own thinking, to engage you more fully with the concerns raised on these pages. You can use a journal, if you like, to write responses to the end-of-chapter questions. Your main goal is for you to figure out where you are, so to speak, and for you to take the next step. That is, figure out where your burning questions lie, and take some steps toward dealing with them. Merely reading a book will not do this for you. Nor will keeping a journal. These are tools to prompt your own initiative. Your initiative is the thing. But the tools are valuable means to that end. A journal can be both an invitation to and a diary of a trip. But the trip is yours.

Get a companion. The best kind of trip is one you take with a friend. I think that is true of the kind of questions you will be addressing in the book. End-of-chapter questions have been written with the idea that you and another might tackle them together, each hearing the other's insights and concerns, encouraging each other in the journey. You may already have someone who is friend-of-your-mind, first hearer of your questions and ideas. You are blessed. It is fine to invite someone whom you have yet to know well to join you in reading this book together. Through it you may gain a friend-of-your-mind that you did not have before. You may choose to converse with a friend or even two, rather than keep a journal.

PART I

Knowing . . .

Knowing
is the responsible human struggle
to rely on clues
to focus on a coherent pattern
and submit to its reality.

1

"Show Your Work"

The Nagging Question: Can We Know God?

"Show your work." Thus read the directions on countless math and chemistry tests. Now that I teach logic, I make tests with the same directions. What does it mean? It means that you get little credit simply for having the right answer.

Can we know God? Many people ask this question. It seems it would be a simple one to answer. Four one-syllable words, not exactly stretching our vocabulary, a question calling for a simple yes or no answer. I could give you a one-word answer to the question *Can we know God?* My answer is *yes*.

But we all know that the question only appears to be a simple one. In reality it is complex and provocative, and much is at stake in its answer. Answering it calls for a book (and a lifetime!), not a bumper sticker.

This book is my showing my work, accounting for my affirmative answer to the question *Can we know God?* This book is written for people who are asking the question and, for whatever reason, desperately need more than the one-word response. Askers of such a question include people who want to know God, as well as people who thought they knew him already. All of us at times can desperately want to know him while feeling unsure of whether or how.

A simple answer can for some people be enough. People who know God and live their lives before him with confidence in his knowing them can and should answer the question with a simple yes, without out feeling that they need to demonstrate their claim. The fact that they have not "shown their work"—reasoned their way through definitions and evidence to conclusions—does not discredit their lived experience. The person who knows God would rightly feel it inappropriate to say that their knowledge of him rests on a reasoned argument. This is not because knowing God is irrational, but because what's rational, on further examination, is different from what we may have expected. That's one of the things I hope to show in this book.

But people confident about their knowing God still benefit from thinking through the basis for their confidence. It is a rich experience to know God. The same experience is enriched further by knowing how you know. The golfer who gets a hole-in-one enjoys a rich experience. The golfer who gets a hole-in-one as a result of well-honed skill has a deeper one, and one upon which he or she can rely with confident hope for the future.

And people confident about knowing God at times lose that confidence and must go back to the basics. (As do golfers!) Crises of one sort or another prompt us to stop and scrutinize what we thought we were confident of. A death or betrayal, a new learning situation, a shift in the philosophical outlook of our culture—these things and others can move us to ask the question again with fresh urgency. In these times, people who ordinarily say they know God can benefit from someone "showing the work" that supports their answer. People who know God and people who know God but struggle with doubt, I hope, will both find this book helpful.

Another group of people settle for a simple answer to the question, Can we know God? They are people who want to blow off the question. Bumper stickers sometimes so trivialize important issues that they let us off the hook. They let us keep living our lives on the surface, dismissing with a breezy "Whatever!" deeper issues about ourselves and the world. Perhaps as you pick this book up you find yourself in the "Whatever!" category, happy to pass by the question. Why, you might be saying, should I bother to ask it?

But let me tantalize you. I'd like to suggest that, no matter who you are and no matter how breezy your "Whatever!" somewhere a quiet voice within you counterpoints with another question, "What if—?" What if there really is more to life? What if a reality outside the reality I make really has the last word? What if that reality includes a God I am responsible to know? If God exists, and I don't know him, I am in big trouble. I am like the villain at the end of the James Bond movie: something I didn't know or plan on finally does me in. If you are a member of the human race, I suggest, the question about God persistently resurfaces in your life. This book, I hope, will heighten your longing to know and help you think it through.

So this book is for people thoughtfully considering the question *Can we know God?* What is at stake in its answer? And what makes it so complex and provocative? Why do we feel the question with rising anxiety?

So much is at stake in the answer because, if people can know God, the next obvious question is what in fact we know about him. If God is, what he is has far-reaching consequences for our lives—who we are, how we live, and what happens after death. Perhaps the simplest way to say it is this: If God is, and he is master of all, then he is master of you and your world. If he isn't, then you are. You might see one or the other alternative as the preferable one. But it's impossible to be indifferent about the choice; it hits just too close to home for comfort.

What makes the question so complex? The question is deceptively simple. It's complex because its simple words have been used to refer to a range of meanings so wide that the alternatives contradict each other. It is impossible to do justice to the question without considering first what *know* means, and what we mean by *God*. Our response to the question will be shaped profoundly by our definition of these terms.

What makes the question *Can we know God?* so provocative? To begin with, there's hardly a consensus on the answer, either for the affirmative or for the negative. And within the camp of those who say yes, no clear consensus can be found concerning the nature of the God we claim to know.

So much seems to challenge an affirmative answer. We're talking, after all, about knowing a being who isn't seen, touched, or heard. If someone reports in our hearing that he or she *did* see, touch, or hear God, we're likely to wonder about the legitimacy of their experience. The philosophical legacy of our times disposes people generally to discredit religious experience in contrast to sense experience, science, and ordinary rationality. In fact, it is quite common these days to discredit all claims to confident knowledge of any sort.

Saying *no* to the question, by the way, requires as much work to be shown as saying *yes*. A general disposition to discredit religious experience rests on just as many answers to other questions. Plus, it is even more difficult to "show the work" if you can't even see what work needs to be shown.

But we can't just blame our difficulties in saying yes to the question on the philosophical legacy of our time. If you will grant for a moment that God exists and that the Bible accurately describes him, then the problem of knowing God is deeper than philosophical. It has to do with something that went wrong that warped our thinking. Human knowing is bent by human rebellion against God. It's like having to show your work on a calculus exam when you've spent your life hiding from math. In addition to talking about what we mean by *God* and what we mean by *know*, the Bible says we also have to consider what we mean by *can!*

If you feel as if you'd really rather duck the question, the way you feel isn't just because the question is complex and provocative. It isn't just because it's downright hard to answer. It's also that you're up against some brokenness or bentness in your life, as am I. The bentness makes you want to run from dealing with the question.

Can we simply avoid answering the question? Can we just suspend judgment on whether we can know God, or whether he exists? Many people try to do this. In fact for centuries now philosophers have touted this approach as the road to tolerance, the one way to avoid frightfully damaging religious wars. But the question refuses to go away. We seem connected to God, in much the same way that we are connected to our parents—the family systems therapists call it emotional fusion. Some people try to deny the connectedness, but the very denial reveals how stuck to their parents they are. (This may be why questions relating to God inflame our emotions.)

That's the negative side of it. The positive side of this question's obstinacy is our very human longing for transcendent reality. We may be bent, but the bentness has not snuffed out our sense of glory. We don't know exactly what we long for; that doesn't seem to stop us from longing for something ultimate. Again, if the Bible is right about who God is and who we are, about how we were made by him but because of our bentness do not recognize him, the fact that we all run in different directions propelled by the same longing for transcendence makes perfect sense.

And that is why the question *Can we know God?* persistently resurfaces in our lives. To live with integrity requires that you and I consider it seriously and offer something more than a bumper-sticker response. I offer this book to prompt and aid your thoughtful effort.

For Further Thought and Discussion

Locate yourself, your beliefs and longings, in light of the alternatives presented in this chapter and in the Foreword. Choose the statements that represent what you think. How does what you think compare to what others around you think? Add any explanation you think is important:

____ I have big questions about whether people can access truth.

____ I don't have any such questions.

____ I think asking such questions is dangerous.

____ I think asking such questions is unnecessary.

___ I am not a Christian.

___ I am considering Christianity.

___ I am a Christian, but I have questions and doubts about knowing God.

___ I am a Christian, and I am confident in knowing and being known by God.

___ I don't care about knowing God.

___ I want to know God.

___ I am still growing up on the outside.

___ I am still growing up on the inside.

There are some circumstances in my life that have prompted me to raise questions about knowing truth and knowing God, such as:

Here is what I think right now about *God:*

Here is what I think right now about *knowing:*

Here is what I think right now about *knowing God:*

Identify your questions. List the questions whose answers you feel you are longing to know. List the things you think people you know are longing to know. Do you think these are questions that this book may help you to address?

2

Let's Talk about Knowing

Thinking about Knowing God, Thinking about Knowing

I said that in order to respond thoughtfully to the question *Can we know God?* we must at least talk about what we mean by *God*, and also what we mean by *know*. In this book I want to think with you about what we mean by *know*.

The Painful Personal Question

I grew up in a home and a church that taught the Bible faithfully, so I can never remember a time when I didn't have a solid concept of God. I knew what I was supposed to know about God. That's why, for me, the live question has always been about how we know. What sense did it make even to talk about God, it seemed, if I didn't have a satisfactory answer about knowing? And questioning knowing as I did, I didn't exactly feel confident that I knew God.

I had questions not only about knowing God. I also had questions about knowing anything. I came of age in a philosophical world wrestling with "our knowledge of the external world," the title of one of early-twentieth-century philosopher Bertrand Russell's books. And I shared with all Westerners a Greek heritage: If ancient Greece was the cradle of Western civilization, I think it fair to say that skepticism was the blanket the baby came wrapped in. How can we be sure we know anything at all?

It can be painful to harbor doubts, especially when you are surrounded, as I was, by a community of dear people whom I felt I would disappoint if I told them. Plus, it seemed that my doubts discredited my claim to know God. Assurance, many believers feel, is a sign of the reality of our being in right relationship with God. I concluded that absence of assurance meant that I was not in right relationship with God. I felt out of step with others; I felt out of step with myself. And, of course, I surmised that my doubts didn't exactly make God happy either. I needed, for my own well-being, to deal with the question of knowing. All this is why, through all the years of my adult life, and now in this book, the question of what we mean by *know* has taken precedence.

At the time, I also thought that I was the only one with the problem. I didn't know in those early years that centuries of thinkers had wondered and written about knowing. When I did find this out, and found out that pursuing this topic is what the discipline of philosophy does, it didn't take me long to jump in.

Since the time that I completed my graduate work in philosophy, the philosophical climate has changed. Sometimes we refer to this as a shift from modernism to postmodernism. Among the many themes we associate with postmodernism is the idea that humans can have no objective truth, that truth is something that each person (or people group) individually determines. It seemed to me that if you don't think you have a truth to know, then you shouldn't have issues about knowing. With this in mind as I approached teaching students two decades younger than myself, I thought that they would not have epistemological issues as I did, or at least not the same issues.

■ "God! I Want to Believe Again, But I Don't Know How!"

I have learned that I was mistaken. The question of knowing is as live now, if not more live, than it was before. A major reason, I believe, is this: It does not sit comfortably with a person to affirm, and try to live, the claim that we have access to no objective (outside of myself) truth. People are implicitly aware that this claim calls for as much justification as the claim that we do have access to objective truth. I need not explain this further at the moment; this book should do the job.

Here's another reason. I have listened to a number of my students talk about themselves, and about their friends. They speak urgently about the need to resolve issues about knowing. I teach students who are Christians and studying theology, who want to help others who are considering Christianity. Although in recent centuries some theologians have tried to say that you can be a Christian without affirming certain things to be true, I (and many others) humbly submit that this is nonsense. Historically, to be a Christian is necessarily to affirm that certain things are true about God, about humans, and about reality. We affirm, for example, the Apostles' Creed: "I believe in God, the Father Almighty, Maker of heaven and earth; and in Jesus Christ, his only Son, our Lord. . . ." We affirm that the Bible is God authoritatively telling us the way things are.

For any person influenced by the postmodernist milieu, then, considering Christianity requires facing questions about knowing. If it ever was just a question of putting your trust in God, for postmodern people the prior question is about putting your trust in the possibility of knowing. Considering Christianity forces people to think about knowing. My young students ask the questions with as much urgency as I did, if not more.

"It started out as a kind of emotional dryness," Michael, one of my students, told me. "I felt as if I wasn't feeling very passionately about things I ought to feel passionately about. I had become a Christian a few years before. I couldn't necessarily deny my faith—my personal experience kept me from that: I had changed so much when I became a Christian. I could see big differences in my life.

"But in this emotionally dry time, I began to ask, What tangible evidence of the truth of Christianity is there in my life? The answers I had given to others now seemed pat. I began to wonder if what I believed was really all a sham— that I went on believing it, not because I knew it was real, but because I couldn't face living without the hope.

"I struggled to account for the disparity of my experience from that of unbelievers. I had a friend, Jonathan, who had struggled with the same questions and had concluded that Christianity was not for him. I felt that I couldn't claim the certainty I needed to have in the face of unbelievers' disagreement. Yet I knew that to settle for thinking that what I believed was private—true just for me, to satisfy my private longing—would torpedo the very thing I believed in."

Michael took a leave of absence from his theological studies because he felt he couldn't continue with integrity unless he settled these questions. He went to Wales and worked on a falcon farm. On a weekend trip to Oxford, he sat in the Eagle and Child, the pub frequented by C. S. Lewis, J. R. R. Tolkien, and the other "Inklings." He contemplated the words of William Butler Yeats:

> Turning and turning in the widening gyre
> The falcon cannot hear the falconer;
> Things fall apart; the centre cannot hold;
> Mere anarchy is loosed upon the world.

In anguish, Michael scrawled these words on the back of a brochure: "I just reread Yeats' *The Second Coming.* I feel like the Falcon. . . . I'm in the Eagle and the Child in Oxford, it's the Inklings old pub. I wish they were here to echo the falconers voice. . . . What do I believe anymore? Why do I believe it? My whole life, since I was fifteen, has been centered on Christianity . . . my ethics, my studies, my taste in Art . . . in music. If I strip all this away . . . remove the peripheral, do I still believe??? If I believe in truth that can be known in part . . . how do we know? What do I do with Jesus? I can't escape the haunting question of that painting from the museum in London where Christ stands with Peter asking him 'who do you say that I am?' The longer I looked at the painting the more I felt like the question was really intended for me." Michael felt faithless, purposeless, and deeply confused—about himself, as well as about God.

Some months later he went home to Georgia and worked as a janitor. "I was wrestling with two big questions at that time," he said. "One was the problem of evil—how can a good God and evil happenings exist in the same reality? The other was about knowledge: How can I know what I think I know? I was looking for certainty; I felt I needed it for intellectual integrity. 'True for me' was not enough; but what else is there? Nor was Pascal's wager satisfactory—the idea that even though we don't know whether Christianity is true, we ought to choose it just to avoid its consequences in case it is."

Michael wrote in his journal, "God! I want to believe again, but I don't know how!"

I write this book about knowing for people like Michael. And for people like me. What is written in this book has pointed the way for me, for Michael, and others.

The Thorny Question of Knowing

Understanding what *knowing* means may actually be more difficult than understanding what *God* means. There certainly are more obvious payoffs for exploring and understanding God. Exploring knowing can be arduous and frustrating. It's like what Saint Augustine said about time—"If I don't think about it, I know what it is, but when you ask me to define it, I can't." We would probably say that we're involved in knowing, every waking hour. But perhaps for precisely that reason it is extremely difficult to put into words what it means to know. The question strikes us simultaneously as both the profoundest and perhaps the silliest.

But for me, figuring out knowing was the crucial missing link. I couldn't settle down to thinking about God, and I couldn't benefit from thinking about God, until I had addressed the question about knowing. I had to ask the profound and silly question. But in dealing with it I found a double payoff: knowing knowing, and knowing God.

I want to explore the human act of knowing. I call this the *epistemic* act. The Greek root of this word means "know"; *epistemology* is the study of how we know. In our day-to-day affairs, we ordinarily talk about knowing math concepts or knowing sports, for example. Obviously in the process we make assumptions about what knowing involves. Epistemology scrutinizes those often hidden assumptions: How does knowledge come to me? What characteristics does a claim to knowledge have to possess in order to be, legitimately, knowledge? How do I tell if a claim is true? What truths can I be sure of? How, bottom line perhaps, do I keep from being mistaken?

I believe that it is tremendously helpful to think about what goes into an epistemic act (and what doesn't). When we do this, we gain a fresh perspective both on knowing and on knowing God. In fact, the best thing I think I can do to encourage you about the prospect of knowing God is to help you think about how you already go about knowing. And I think you'll find that even as you think about the one you will easily be encouraged about the other.

For Further Thought and Discussion

Tell your own story. In this chapter you have heard portions of two people's stories. What is your story? Write it in your journal or tell it to a friend.

- What events in your life have raised burning questions for you?
- What different questions have you asked at what points in your story?
- Where were you when you felt the questions most strongly?
- What have you done to pursue them?

- What books or people or experiences have helped you along the way?
- What conclusions or working maxims have you reached?

Listen to your friend's story. Compare your story to mine, to Michael's, to your friend's.

- Features in common:
- Points of contrast:

How does hearing others' stories help?

Mark your progress: If your story is a quest or a journey, take a guess at where you are along the way. If on a scale of 1 to 10, 1 represents the beginning of your journey and 10 represents its end, at what number do you think you are now?

3

The Dangling Carrot of Certainty

What We Think about Knowing, and Why

Know is an odd word! Suppose I say that I *know* that my husband is at the hardware store. Doesn't it seem as if he absolutely has to be there? Suppose I find out later that he really was at the bookstore. Then I have to fix what I said before: I no longer say that I *knew* he was at the hardware store; I say I *thought* he was at the hardware store. *Know* is a success word: when we use it we imply that we were successful at getting the truth right. So we have thought that knowing something means that what we claim to know can't be wrong or we cannot doubt—that it is *infallible,* or *certain.* For knowledge to *be* knowledge at all, it must be infallible or certain. Otherwise it is opinion, or belief, but not knowledge.

Plus, people have felt that for a truth claim to be *worth* anything at all, it must be infallible or certain, or provably connected to such certainties. What good is a truth claim, a statement that claims for itself that it is true, if it might turn out to be false? How does a claim that is less than certain anchor us and enable us to navigate the unknowns of each day of our lives? Infallibility and certainty are huge issues when we think about knowing. Other words that have been used to describe these central features of knowledge are *necessity,* that the truth claim can't possibly be otherwise, and *universality,* that the truth claim would be true for everybody.

If knowledge, to be knowledge and to be worth anything, must be infallible and certain, the next obvious question is, Which truth claims, if any, actually make the cut? And how is it decided what makes the cut? What do I have to do as a knower to insure that the claims I embrace have made the cut? How do I avoid being wrong?

All of us want to be sure. I want to be sure about the information in our mortgage contract. We want the jet pilot to be sure of his or her measurements and readings. We want our teachers to be sure of what they make us learn. We want to be sure about the person we marry or the business partnership we arrange. We want ourselves and other drivers to be sure when they gauge the distance between one and another car. We want to be sure about God's existence or nonexistence. Especially in areas in which a lot is at stake in the truth of our claims, we want to be sure.

Some of us want more than just to be sure; we want to be shown. Suppose that you live in the state of Missouri, so to speak. Missouri is the Show Me State. Presumably that's because Missourians don't take your word for it; you have to prove to them why it's so. Suppose you are surrounded by belligerent Missourians who answer your every statement with "Oh yeah? Show me." (Not that I've met too many belligerent Missourians!) Suppose they tacitly or explicitly suggest that there isn't anything you can say that survives the knowledge cut. People who believe that knowledge isn't possible are called *skeptics.* If you are faced with defending your claim to knowledge in an atmosphere of skepticism, you are going to feel extra pressure to undergird your claim with so firm and indisputable a rationale that even the skeptics will be proven wrong.

▋ Skepticism to Certainty to Skepticism: Cycle 1

In light of all this, let's take a really short look at the history of Western philosophy. I want to give you a sense of what people in this tradition have thought knowledge must be like. And I want, second, to show how connected our idea of knowledge has been to skepticism. I think we can sketch out two huge cycles moving away from and back to skepticism, the classical cycle and the modern cycle. Having exhausted the second cycle, we stand as a culture on the brink of an unavoidable decision but with no obvious alternative to skepticism.

My point is going to be this: If knowledge is as philosophers have thought for centuries, if our efforts to know have certainty as their uncompromising ideal, then skepticism seems the inevitable alternative. But our lived experience witnesses powerfully that this cannot be. So maybe we need to revise how we think about knowledge.

The Greek philosopher Plato (404–384 B.C.), disciple of Socrates, faced a skeptical milieu. Some people were teaching that there is no objective knowledge. Protagoras had uttered his still-famous aphorism, "Man is the measure of all things." Teachers called Sophists were offering their services for hire to up-and-coming Greek citizens, not to teach them knowledge, but in the absence of knowledge to teach people how to persuade others to give them what they want. Then Socrates, Plato's beloved teacher, was executed on the charge that he was corrupting the youth of Athens. Had he not already thought otherwise, Plato had all the motivation he needed to prove that some things are wrong and others are right, that infallible and certain knowledge is possible and critically important to society. So was born Western philosophy, with Plato its acknowledged father. But the chick had to peck out of an eggshell of skepticism.

Plato followed Socrates' lead in developing the idea that the key ingredient that makes knowledge knowledge is the thing that we are knowing, the object of knowledge. For knowledge to be knowledge, certain and free of mistake, we have to access by means of it ultimate realities that are permanent, unchanging originals. We see horses. But to know the concept of horse, you have to figure out what it is that all horses have in common, what are the essential features a certain item has to have in order to be a horse. What you are doing is developing a definition of "horse." When you have specified that set of essential features, that essence, you are in touch with the proper object of knowledge. The essence isn't identical to any horse you see. It is separate from the horse, and spiritual, not material. But the essence horse is more important and, Plato said, more real than any horse you see. For any horse you see to be a horse, it must be patterned after the essential, archetypal horse. Plato called these essences *arches,* or forms. And truth claims that access the rational essences of things are thereby anchored by a justification that makes those claims certain knowledge.

Plato's disciple, Aristotle, also tutor to Alexander the Great, agreed that what makes knowledge knowledge, certain and infallible, was that it specifically expressed the essential features of the object in question. But he didn't think that this essence existed separately from the object itself. What sense did it make to think that there was another horse in addition to all the horses that there are in the world? What sense did it make to think that the very things that make a horse a horse are not really in the horse?

If you look at Raphael's famous painting, *The School of Athens,* you see at the center of a people-filled basilica two men walking together and talking. One is older, the other is younger. The older one is pointing up; the younger one is stretching his hand out horizontally. The older one is Plato; the younger is Aristotle. Raphael represented them disagreeing about the location of these essences. They also disagreed about how we access them. But they agreed that the proper object of knowledge, the thing we must access for our claims to count as knowledge—the foundation that alone makes knowledge certain and infallible—and possible—is the forms. And they agreed, even more fundamentally, that for knowledge to be knowledge it has to be certain and infallible. They agreed that this sort of knowledge was crucial to life and society, and that it is possible, even though difficult, to access it.

There is much to be gained from studying Plato and Aristotle, even if you think that in some key respects they were mistaken. To understand them is to understand our entire Western legacy, and to understand ourselves. Much about your outlook is the way it is, if you are a Westerner, because of Plato and Aristotle.

Centuries of thought from their time forward worked to explain more fully how essences anchor our knowledge, and what we must do to access them. This discussion in the Middle Ages came to be known as the problem of universals (another word for essences or forms). The problems plaguing this approach gradually came to outweigh the advantages. Essences taken as objective realities actually came to impede the advance of knowledge, to stand in the way of our exploration.

When the critics of universals won the upper hand, the entire Western philosophical outlook began to change. We moved from the classical to the modern, as these milieus are sometimes called. Modern approaches are clearly detectable in the late 1400s and early 1500s.

This shift must have been devastating to live through. Every time I teach the history of philosophy and I get to this part of the story, I feel very sad. It's not that I agree with everything about the classical worldview. It's just that I can imagine that it felt safe and workable. The world was familiar, known, and comfortingly the same. There wasn't much to talk about once you knew the essence of horses. What's more, the world had a comforting connection with God. For it had come to be widely held that the essences were ideas in the mind of God. He guaranteed their unbending nature because they were his thoughts after which he had patterned the world when he made it. And of course they were absolute truth. But when all this was questioned, the world must have come to feel an alien, impersonal place. You couldn't take it for granted that you knew what a horse was, or what God was thinking. You couldn't feel as if you really knew horses. You no longer had an inside grasp on what they are. And it was no longer so obvious, from the philosopher's point of view, how to access God.

■ Skepticism to Certainty to Skepticism: Cycle 2

When the reality of an objective anchor for our knowledge was called into question, the very possibility of knowledge was once again called into question. Once again there developed an aura of skepticism. René Descartes, thought of as the father of modern philosophy, was writing in the mid-1600s. He wrote to propose a sure and certain foundation for knowledge, in the face of yet another major skeptical challenge. He rejected the comforting but problematic essences of the classical approach. He had to find a new foundation for certain and infallible knowledge.

What was different about the modern approach to knowledge? Where Plato and company had thought that the anchor and guarantee of knowledge lay outside ourselves in the world around us, modern thinkers postulated that it lay in the knower's mind. Descartes spoke of clear and distinct ideas (meaning ideas in our mind): ideas that the knower is certain about, that can't possibly be false. We tidy them into existence through rigorous efforts to reject unsupported opinions, to break complex ideas down into simple ones, to examine them one by one, and to make sure everything is as orderly as possible. What guarantees certain knowledge is not in our world but in our minds.

Modern philosophy has been ringing changes on this theme through centuries, well into the twentieth. Bertrand Russell, whom I mentioned before, was an influential modern philosopher, one of many. He, like many others, attempted to express what criteria a knowledge claim had to meet in order for it to be certain and infallible knowledge. He called our most basic mental ideas sense data, little idea bits small enough to match and have been caused by our individual sense experiences. Russell himself could see big problems with this approach. How do we know that there is an external world beyond our sense data, for example? How can we be certain that our sense data match anything? But modernists pressed on because they believed that knowledge was possible, and because they had no viable alternative model.

■ Skepticism to . . . What?: Starting Cycle 3

Another shift in philosophical outlook has engulfed us. If you are over thirty-five, you know what it is to have a foot on either side of the wave. If you are younger, you may only grasp the newer side of the wave.

What set the shift in motion? Modern philosophers never came up with an iron-clad specimen of what they thought they had to have: ideas in the mind clear and distinct enough to support the very truth claims they believed ought to survive the cut as knowledge—such as statements about the physical world. The mental ideas that they presumed to be the very anchor of our knowledge actually cut us off from the world. Plus, over the modernist period, philosophers who agreed that the mind's thoughts anchored knowledge nevertheless offered proposals disturbingly inconsistent with each other. People became increasingly aware of how presumptuous it was to think that everybody's mind works the way Descartes's (or ours) does. Plus, we gradually had to admit that every knower's interests and culture and outlook significantly shape what he or she is knowing. (Thank you, Friedrich Nietzsche.) How can there be certain, infallible, objective knowledge when what we claim is true seems to be determined by subjective factors such as our cultural upbringing or our personal ambitions? These things all threaten to undermine any claim to knowledge.

In this shift away from modernism we all feel the press to admit skepticism, and we reap the rootlessness of a shattered worldview. How can we know anything at all? Nothing is certain but uncertainty. While this represents an egregious oversimplification, postmodernism is this newest capitulation to skepticism. There is no absolute truth, no metanarrative, no single grand story, no single way-things-are. This is certainly skepticism.

Will we this time settle down to skepticism? It's not, after all, a new idea. Why didn't it stick the first or second time? Will it stick this time, now that we are so much more superior and up to the challenge of rootlessness (as some might say)?

Why Skepticism Doesn't Seem like a Fit

I do not believe that skepticism is the default mode for humans. For one thing, we are bothered by the inconsistency of saying that we know that nothing can be known, or that it is true that there is no truth.

But I believe also that we all feel within ourselves the misfit of skepticism, as Cinderella's stepsisters did the glass slipper. (And you might say that for centuries we have been cutting off our big toe to make the slipper fit.) For knowing nothing at all, you and I seem to know quite a lot. Or at least we seem to live like it—that is, when it isn't more personally advantageous to be skeptics. Vast portions of our lives and jobs and society are devoted to information, learning, and discovery. What's more, we continually make advances from unknowing to knowing, whether in the classroom or the science lab or in the ordinary

31

affairs of life. This is the story of our lives. This belies skepticism. We've felt compelled to call ourselves skeptics in the name of integrity. But all along we felt the inauthenticity of such a label, since our human lives, just because they are human lives, are a tapestry of acts of knowing.

Classicists, modernists, and skeptics have agreed: For knowledge to be knowledge, it has to be characterized by certainty and infallibility, necessity, universality. They have struggled to formulate foolproof criteria for certainty and knowledge, and many, not just the skeptics, have admitted that their results were less than satisfactory. The skeptics differ in this respect: the concessions they feel they need to make in defining knowledge are ultimately insurmountable. So while these groups agree about the ideal of knowledge, they have disagreed as to whether such knowledge was possible.

And it isn't just the philosophers. People without philosophical training have ideas about knowledge. Generally people think that knowledge has to be something you are sure of, that can't be wrong, or it isn't knowledge. And people disagree, at least on the surface, regarding whether knowledge is possible. And now, at this juncture in our developing Western heritage, even people without philosophical training feel with the philosophers that the classical and the modernist approaches have been effectively dismantled. Nobody can relate to essences, and the idea of ideas in the mind is beginning to fall by the wayside, too. That leaves us with skepticism.

If the remaining alternative, skepticism, isn't a fit, then something may be wrong with the assumptions that have shaped both it and classical and modern philosophy. Maybe we need to rethink what we mean by knowledge. The movie *Star Trek II: The Wrath of Khan* begins with a candidate for starship captain taking the Kobiashi-Maru test in the starship simulator. The test is unpassable, and she experiences appropriate consternation. Later, during a quiet moment in prison with the legendary starship captain James T. Kirk, she asks how he managed to pass that test. His answer is classic—and bears on our discussion: "I reprogrammed the simulator's computer!"

Some things in particular tip us off to the misfit of skepticism, and to the ideal of knowledge anchored in some privileged strata of certainties. The ideal of certainty in knowledge is this: I must accept as true only those claims of which I am rationally certain, having no shadow of doubt. The search for such certainty, we have found in the centuries of our Western tradition, has led the stalwart to part with even the dearest of the commitments to which we might be naturally inclined. Platonists parted with their senses' perception, reinterpreted as so many toy objects and their shadows on the wall of Plato's allegorical cave. Descartes, in pursuit of an Archimedean anchor of certainty, parted not only with the fireside perceivings of his senses but even with something more dear than this to this mathematician, his mathematics. Russell parted with his certainty that his sense data represented an external world, quite a problem of induction for someone who believed in the progress of science. Dismissing the findings of our senses and the reliability of an external world qualifies as toe cutting, if anything does.

Driven to attain an ideal of certainty, thinkers have over the centuries tightened the parameters of "proper" knowledge so restrictively that what was left was at best truisms, or so minimalistic and private that all the mess of reality has been squeezed out of them. The work of David Hume, a philosopher in the 1700s, climaxed a progression of efforts to eliminate statements for which we have no justification, including whether I perceive myself perceiving. He decided that you and I just perceive our perceptions. He did not think we perceived causal connections, either, but rather concurrent or successive perceptions. He responded to this frightful plight by having a party and playing backgammon— a healthy if inconsistent concession to the connections he denied. Analytic philosophy in the twentieth century at its outset restricted knowledge to logical truths ("Either it is raining or it is not raining.") and minimalistically expressed reports of atoms of sense experience ("This here red."), and any statements that could be derived from combinations of these. And it is still very much a part of the Western philosophical tradition to accept as knowledge only those statements that can be fully justified, and thus to try to determine what kind of justification would be foolproof. While many noted and wrestled with the restrictiveness of the ideal, they did not surrender the attempt to reach it, and many did surrender big toes such as human personhood, art, religion, and ethics.

If we limit "knowledge" to statements that meet this standard of certainty, we end up having to say that we know precious little. Even if we could attain certain and infallible knowledge, that "knowledge" would be so sterile and disconnected from both the knower and the known reality as to be useless. Even if you grant, for example, the legitimacy of statements such as "This here red," all that tells you about is what is inside your head; it offers you no access to the world outside it.

The Western tradition, thanks to its very verbal source (Plato, you might say, made defining terms the essence of philosophy), has unquestioningly assumed that knowledge is limited to what can be put into words and justified. We think of knowledge as statements and proof. But here's another indicator of the misfit of this approach: If scientists had been so limited, no scientific discovery ever would have taken place. If students had been restricted to statements and proof, no learning ever would have taken place. For whatever the discovering and learning processes end up with, with respect to statements and certainty, they cannot possibly begin with statements and certainty. How can you verbalize your cluelessness? How can you verbalize your clues at the point at which you are guided by them? How can you make justified statements about what you have yet to learn or discover? But learning and discovery occur regularly. Therefore . . . write the conclusion yourself.

What of the ideal of certainty itself? If I must accept as true only those claims of which I am certain, what about the claim that I must accept as true only those claims of which I am certain? Am I certain of it? What reasons would I use to prove it? The ideal does not even meet its own standard. It is a claim of which I cannot be certain. We might say that it is an expression of faith.

The donkey plods hopefully after a carrot dangling from a stick before him. Certainty—that fat old carrot that's been tantalizing us for centuries—is a misguided ideal. The donkey would be far better rewarded if he got to his own carrot than we have been or ever would be by reaching ours.

■ What Now?

Philosophers from well back into the nineteenth century, disturbed by adverse consequences of the modernist model of knowledge, have been attempting to revise this faulty conception of knowledge, and have made very insightful proposals. With several decades of retrospect, the similarities and significance of these efforts become more marked. In our shift away from modernism, whole domains of human experience I believe have the prospect of being restored to us.

But these revisions divide from one another over the question of truth and reality. Is it, or is it not, appropriate to talk of truth and reality? The central thrust of what we call postmodernism would have us reject the ideas of truth and reality. That is why I suggest that postmodernism calls us to skepticism. And if we are being asked to settle for skepticism, I believe our search for a workable model of human knowing must still be continued, for we are being asked to settle for that which is untrue to our very selves. I believe that postmodern voices offer skepticism about truth and reality because, growing as they do out of the stump of Western philosophy, they have yet to recognize and accredit a couple of features of human experience and knowing. These features restore to us what inside of ourselves we cannot deny: the hope, and the longing, to engage the real, along with our felt sense that we do so. Those features are what I want to tell you about in this book.

34

If skepticism doesn't fit our human experience, and if the models of knowledge don't offer a workable explanation, it's time to rethink their common assumption about what knowledge is. It's time for a different approach, something that goes deeper than yea or nay. It's time to take a look at what we already are doing as humans when we are engaged in knowing, and revise our conception in light of our experience. And when we do this, what we find also helps us when it comes to thinking about how we know God.

For Further Thought and Discussion

Identify truth claims. A *truth claim* is a statement that claims for itself that it is true. A truth claim can actually be true or false. Think of three truth claims. Make them statements that you actually believe are true. For fun, pick them from different areas of your experience—family life, nature, and epistemology, for example.

Identify their support. For each of the truth claims you listed, tell what you would say if someone were to ask you why you think it is true. You may find that you have a sequence of reasons. Spell out the sequence.

The answers we give to such a question reveal the reasons, or the support, or the justification that we have for a truth claim. How do they feel to you? Do they feel like anchors for your truth claims, for example?

Evaluate the strength of your support. For each truth claim and its support, say how solid you think the support is. Use percentages, where a percentage closer to 0 represents weak support and a percentage closer to 100 represents solid support.

Evaluate the quality of your support. Think about your answers so far.

- Do you think that different kinds of support can be given for the same truth claim?
- Do you think some kinds of support or justification might be superior to others?
- What would be an example of an inferior kind of support? Here's one example: choosing a color of paint recommended to you by a color-blind person.
- What would be an example of a superior kind of justification?
- What features would characterize a superior kind of justification?

35

These are the kinds of questions that philosophers are wrestling with when they make proposals about knowing. Plato suggested that truth claims are like statues so lifelike that they walk around. They need to be anchored so that they don't walk around. Good justification gives us such an anchor, he said. So we have to think about what counts as good justification.

Class the recommendations of our Western heritage.

- In the classical period, the anchor of a solid justification for truth claims was:
- In the modern period, the anchor of a solid justification for truth claims was:
- Can you relate to either or both or neither of these proposals?
- Are there any alternatives you can think of to these proposed anchors?

Consider skepticism. Are you a skeptic? Why or why not? Do you think that skepticism is a reasonable stance to take in life?

4

Let Me Introduce You to My Auto Mechanic

Ordinary, Everyday Acts of Knowing

I want to tell you about my auto mechanic, Jeff. I know him because his mother used to be secretary to the president of the seminary where my husband and I teach. When we first came eleven years ago to this place, Jeff was fixing cars in his parents' garage. Everybody I met at the seminary used him because he would come pick up the cars from the seminary and return them there when they were fixed.

Later on, Jeff bought a nearby gas station. He has a gas station of the sort I remember from childhood but you don't see very often now: one that you can drop into with a problem, and there is somebody there who knows about cars who can fix you up and get you back on the road. I've actually done that a couple times with Jeff. One time I coasted in with my lights dimming and my alternator dying. I was on the way to a concert with my daughter; I made it to the concert as the conductor took the stand.

Jeff and his staff have fixed our cars for eleven years now. Actually, I've found, the few times I've poked my head in the car bays, I only occasionally see Jeff.

Last time I was there, I saw four other people working on cars, and Jeff was nowhere to be seen. Yet I refer to the entire operation as Jeff's.

He's bought a couple of our old cars, fixed them up, and resold them. He's advised us on the purchase of a new one. Some people in the seminary community have said to me, "I never pick my own new car; I just tell Jeff to find me one! I buy what he chooses."

Here are some other things I know about Jeff and his family. His mom, June, was the most easygoing secretary I ever knew. She always made you feel like you were important enough for her to take whatever time it took to listen to you and help you. But she always got things done speedily and reliably. She had been secretary for the forty years of the seminary's existence. In that time the seminary grew from zero enrollment to several hundred.

Jeff, she told me once, always insists on pumping gas for his mom. When his dad, Bill, retired, Bill went to work for his son getting cars to and from the seminary.

Jeff's family attends the same church as have the seminary's three presidents. Jeff married one of the president's daughters. Shari's too sweet for words. She taught grade school, but now she stays home with their children. Shari's dad, the seminary's last president, is a good friend of mine. I helped throw him a surprise fiftieth birthday party. Jeff has two brothers that I know of; one is a lawyer, and one studied at the seminary and is now a pastor. All I know about his family is good.

I don't really see Jeff much. My husband usually drives the car that needs fixing to work, and when he comes home with it, it is fixed. Our checkbook takes a nosedive (especially when it's my old Taurus that needs work), but the checkbook hemorrhages less than if we were making payments on a new car, and I get around town fine in my old one. It clunks rather dreadfully, because it needs new struts, Jeff says. But he says I'm not injuring anything by letting it go, and he knows I need to conserve funds.

I've had only one person complain to me about Jeff. She said she felt as if when she took her car to him, more things got fixed than she thought needed fixing, and she would be out comparably more money than she had planned. I give Jeff the benefit of the doubt. One person's *picky* is another person's *thorough*, I think to myself. But I also think to myself, maybe I'm paying a little extra, but I feel I can rely on him completely.

I've just told you almost everything I know about Jeff. I probably know him better than most people know their mechanics. I may have greater reason to trust him implicitly. But when it comes to car know-how, I'd trust Jeff sooner than I'd even trust my own senses. And I can't think of anyone I'd trust more, except maybe the *Car Talk* guys (Saturday mornings on National Public Radio). But even there I don't know as much about their family's character.

■ Ordinary Acts of Knowing

I tell you all this because I want you to think with me about the epistemic act of knowing my auto mechanic. I want to suggest in this book that knowing God is like knowing your auto mechanic.

To put it more generally, knowing God involves an epistemic act that has the same basic features that our ordinary, workaday, epistemic acts do. And, contra the skeptics, we do have ordinary, workaday, epistemic acts.

Think of examples of your own epistemic acts as you read on. Knowing what these words mean; knowing that your roommate is at the library; knowing that $E = mc^2$; knowing that you (according to your doctor) have a herniated disk; knowing your baby sister—all these and a myriad more epistemic acts layer up to fill our waking hours. What is knowing all about?

Please don't take my analogy to be saying that God is like my auto mechanic, or vice versa! While there are some similarities (keeping his word, for example), that is not my point. My point is that the epistemic act by which we know the one is fundamentally the same kind of act by which we know the other.

Nor do I mean to suggest that it is no more rewarding or life changing or important to know God than it is for me to know Jeff. I'm simply talking about the act of knowing. Knowing God involves life-wide consequences. Knowing Jeff doesn't. Knowing God involves far greater reward, but it also involves far greater risk.

Perhaps you don't trust your auto mechanic the way I trust mine. Maybe you are a bit suspicious of his claims. But, you see, suspicion is still an act of knowing. Plus, this dynamic is a familiar one for some people when it comes to knowing God.

You may be protesting: "But you can't touch God! You can touch your auto mechanic! The analogy doesn't hold water! I can know an auto mechanic. I have no clue who God is." You're right: I could drive down to Jeff's garage and touch him. I can't do that with God. I think this will be helped as we talk about what goes on in the ordinary act of knowing, and what doesn't. Is touching, for example, necessary to knowing?

Let's also clarify what can be known of God if you do know him. If what the Bible says about God is true, knowing God involves, in part, knowing someone who has been here tangibly in the past, has told us about himself, who has gone away and promised to return. We are very much in an in-between time. The Bible speaks of our loving him whom we have not seen. It talks about our knowing now "in part," seeing "but a poor reflection as in a mirror," but then knowing "face to face," "fully, even as we are fully known." Comparing apples and apples, this epistemic act of knowing God now compares more to, say, Jeff's mom telling me that he has gone to Europe for a visit, but that he promised to fix my car when he gets back. Under such circumstances, it would be ludicrous to claim that I can drive down to Jeff's gas station this minute and touch him.

There is one thing that queers the deal when it comes to knowing God, one thing that doesn't affect us so much when it comes to knowing auto mechanics. According to the Bible, as I said before, we're talking about knowing someone who made us but whom we no longer recognize because of our bentness. That makes knowing God truly a lot more difficult than knowing our auto mechanic. I think I can show you, however, that although the bentness of human rebellion badly warps the act of knowing God, it does not change its structural similarity, as an act of knowing, to knowing your auto mechanic. And that, in this book, is my point.

I am going to be talking a lot about knowing my auto mechanic! I do that not because knowing auto mechanics is so special. I do it to stand for every single ordinary act of human knowing. I chose it because it was ordinary and everyday. I could have chosen knowing a good strawberry or the vintage of a wine, knowing that you left your credit card at the department store, or knowing the square footage of the yard you want to fertilize. Don't fixate on auto mechanics (although I admit you have every reason to in this book!); the book isn't about knowing them, but about knowing anything. Talking about Jeff I hope makes it concrete: All of life is knowing. Let's not restrict knowing to the ivory tower.

For Further Thought and Discussion

Find your own example. Think of someone you know, perhaps someone who has come to mind as I have described what I know of my auto mechanic.

- Name that person.
- Describe some things you know about that person.
- Describe how you support what you believe about that person.
- Describe how knowing what you know about this person impacts your actions.
- Does thinking about this kind of experience shed any light for you on what knowing is like or what knowing God is like?

5

Knowing God Is Like
Knowing Your Auto Mechanic

The Problem of Saying that Knowing God is NOT Like Knowing Your Auto Mechanic

I want to say in this book that knowing God is like knowing your auto mechanic. It's a somewhat amusing proposal, but one that offers tremendous hope. In fact we do know our auto mechanic. If it can be shown that knowing God involves the kind of knowing that we already do, then, yes, we can (and do) know God.

■ "Faith" and "Reason"

Some people have felt that if people can know God, it would have to be by a fundamentally different kind of knowing from the ordinary, workaday, know-your-mechanic kind of knowing. The ultimate things of life, including something so superior as God, simply can't be captured in words and by reason. To try to talk about God, to express him in propositions, is not to know him. He simply surpasses words. We cannot exhaust his reality in a neatly deduced human system.

People who think this way usually say there is a different sort of knowing. It's often mystical or intuitive. They say it is above reason, above rational knowing. It sounds profoundly spiritual, a human act befitting the most ultimate reality of God. We have had mystics as long as we have had talk of rationality.

Plotinus, for example, a neo-Platonist philosopher who lived around A.D. 250, believed that the ultimate reality is the One. It is beyond anything we can put into words. It can be accessed only in the rare moment of ecstatic union. Similar ideas can be found in Eastern thought.

In the Middle Ages, Christian thinkers came to distinguish between faith and reason. Many different things have been meant by these terms, and the debate is as lively now as it was then. However, some people have understood faith and reason to be two different sources of truth about God. Faith would yield belief in God; reason would yield knowledge of God. If you *believe* God exists on the basis of what the Bible says or the church teaches, that's certainly adequate for being saved. But if you have rationally demonstrated that God exists, then you can say that you *know* that God exists. You no longer say that you believe that God exists. Knowledge or reason, when it can be had, replaces belief or faith.

In later centuries, the search for certain foundations in knowledge, combined with growing rejection of church authority as a viable foundation, led philosophers to draw ever more restrictively the boundaries or limits of knowledge. You can only have knowledge that begins with sense experience, empiricists and Kantians said. That means that only sense-based science counts as knowledge. Other domains of human experience don't even count as knowledge: art, ethics, and history were excluded as much as was religion. Immanuel Kant believed that, in restricting knowledge, he was "making room for faith." It sounds noble and religious. I think it was deadly.

Artists reacted in a movement known as romanticism. If that's what knowledge is, if science is all there is to human knowledge, then there has to be something better than rationality and knowledge that is more important to the broader expanses of human experience. The artist mystically or intuitively accesses those ultimate regions that transcend limited, rational, not-really-human knowledge. As a result of this great divide, it remains difficult for scientists and artists to believe that they inhabit the same world as each other. This is unfortunate.

The same divorce can be seen in developments in religion. In the last couple of centuries, some theologians have argued that we must pare Christianity down to its tangible, rational, scientific aspects, jettisoning the "incredible" and retaining only the "credible" portions of Christianity. This approach continues to surface in contemporary theology. Another approach has agreed similarly to a boundary between rational knowing and something that isn't knowing, but has developed the idea that we should place religion outside rational knowing. What they say sounds, in this respect, like Plotinus. It is attractive because it sounds so respectful of God's greatness and his superrational importance in our lives. Both approaches, I hope you see, grow out of some assumptions about what knowledge is and what it isn't.

One of the Bible verses that has been quoted to support this idea says, "'For my thoughts are not your thoughts, neither are your ways my ways,' declares the LORD. 'As the heavens are higher than the earth, so are my ways higher than your ways and my thoughts than your thoughts.'" People who cite these verses to show that we can't know God rationally have missed its point in the context of the passage: God is not like us, not because he is above our knowing, but because he shows mercy (we don't, always) and because his words accomplish what he means them to accomplish (ours don't, always—just try telling your kid to clean up his or her room!). The whole point of the passage is that he means us to seek him and his mercy (which assumes that he thinks we can know him).

I agree wholeheartedly that there are aspects of human knowing that cannot be put into words, as you will see. But I want to show you that this is as true about knowing auto mechanics as it is about knowing God. And I don't believe that we need to be mystical about it, for when we see what goes on in human knowing, we can acknowledge and describe these beyond-words aspects in a more helpful way. But I think it has been a dangerous, damaging mistake to postulate that there is a kind of nonrational knowing by means of which we access God.

■ A Problematic Dichotomy

One automatic, unfortunate consequence of saying that we access God in some way other than knowledge, by faith as opposed to reason, for example, is that faith and its objects inevitably get discredited as something inferior. Reason trumps faith, say medieval scholars. None of our attempts to say that faith is superior have kept us from feeling that when all is said and done, reason is superior. After all, if words and rationality lie on the side of ordinary knowledge, these tools cannot be used to say anything about religious experience. Who would not be compelled, in the name of survival, to anchor most of his or her efforts on the side of the rational? To allow the assumption that you can't know God but can apprehend him in some nonrational way is to be forced to conclude that you can't know God.

We get some of this pressure nowadays, when the generally expressed attitude is that religion is a private affair. It's quite convenient for unbelievers to have a button to push that says, "God can't be known in rational propositions. But that means he can't be talked about, either, and so I shouldn't be expected to listen." We need to get rid of that button.

I mean to unwire the button by saying, "It's not just knowing God that can't be done entirely in rational propositions, with certain and infallible knowledge. We can't and don't know our auto mechanic this way either. And knowing God is like knowing your auto mechanic."

Centuries of Western philosophical thought have labored to build an ever more impregnable wall separating reason and faith, between infallible, certain, rational knowledge and anything that would dilute it or compromise it. I've already said that within the wall, our misguided model has meant that no knowledge of anything valuable ends up making the cut. These self-defeating models of how and what we know come to bear little relationship to ordinary life and knowing, and they prompt us to flirt once more with skepticism even though we cannot affirm this with integrity.

I believe that the presence of the wall separating faith and reason and the misguided model of knowledge on the one side of the wall are integrally connected with each other. To put it in an oversimplified but nevertheless helpful way: The ideal of certainty refuses to countenance features of knowing that we might class as faith. The misguided ideal itself prompts the wall-building. And the wall, in turn, leads to certainty's self-defeat. The wall keeps out just the elements of knowing that undergird all knowing, without which our attempts are either illicit or fruitless. We cannot afford to let this situation persist. The wall must be breached. And this will lead not to the dilution of knowledge but to our proper and transforming understanding of it. And that's why I feel it is important and strategic to say that knowing God is like knowing your auto mechanic.

Our only hope lies in reuniting these domains. It is our only hope not simply for the sake of justifying claims to know God. It is also our only hope for having any knowledge at all. The well-entrenched misperception about the nature of knowledge, one that divorces "proper" knowledge from its inarticulable roots, has in fact led to the widespread skepticism and relativism of our time. *Both* sides of the presumed dichotomy—both faith and reason—face death by absurdity apart from this reconciliation.

It's not that actual human knowing, of both auto mechanics and God, ever has ground to a halt. It's that our accounts of ordinary knowledge and of religious understanding, if constructed to exclude each other, self-destruct. It's that the models haven't fit what we actually do, and they've blinded us to what is actually going on when we know something. In fact we live and know successfully only by operating unconsciously in denial of our culture's prevailing epistemic constructs.

All our efforts will be significantly and effectively advanced if we accurately represent what is going on, and then live in light of our understanding. We need to rethink how it is that we know, starting from the ordinary epistemic experiences of our lives. In this way I believe we will gain insight that will bring healing and hope to our knowing—whether of auto mechanics or of God.

For Further Thought and Discussion

Think about your experience of knowing God.

- Briefly describe your own religious experience.
- What do you believe about how people can know God?
- What justification do you have for thinking this?

In particular, here are some things to think about:

- Do people know God by reason or by faith or by some combination of these? How do you define *reason?* How do you define *faith?*
- Is knowing God like knowing your auto mechanic? What are some similarities and some differences?
- Do you or people around you feel that what you believe about religious things is a private matter? How does this affect what you think about knowing God?

Think about other things you know. Are there faith aspects to other truth claims besides religious ones? Give some examples.

6

Oh! I See It!

Key Features of the Act of Knowing

Have you attempted to do one of those Magic Eye 3-D pictures? You are given a picture that is a complex, minute, computer-generated pattern of colors and figures. The directions tell you to hold the picture close to your face, and then move it slowly away. This exercise enables you to make your eyes focus beyond the surface of the picture. The end result, you are told, is that out of the picture will emerge three-dimensional objects—let's say dolphins.

If you have ever succeeded at one of these, you can testify to your own immense satisfaction and delight at pulling it off. I call this the "Oh! I see it!" moment. I've had it myself, and I've watched others have it. I first encountered 3-D pictures in a display case in the St. Louis airport. Believe me, an entire group of strangers was struggling and squealing together at their success! And I will never forget a hilarious birthday party where the party principal received a card with a 3-D picture. I remember an exceptionally large man sitting on the floor, repeatedly and frustratedly holding the card up to his nose and moving it away. And I remember the Christians present comparing the card experience to coming to know God.

The Magic Eye act has three stages: looking at the picture, struggling to look through it at something as yet unknown, and looking through the picture at the three-dimensional image. The struggle and the switch that prefaces our see-ing the dolphins reveal a kind of toggling, at some point in time or over a period of time, from one way of viewing the picture to another way of viewing the pic-ture. We move from looking at the particulars to looking through them at a far-ther focus, relying on them to see something else that bears little resemblance to them.

Once we have first figured out how to see the dolphins, our continuing to see them has a similar, three-faceted structure. We don't leave the particulars of the picture's surface behind; we rely on them to focus beyond them. The par-ticulars now deserve to be called clues, or *subsidiaries*. We are aware of them, but only as we move ourselves through them and by means of them to grasp a farther focus. Some of the picture's particulars now form part of the dolphins; others we now see as part of the background to the dolphins.

Actually, the particulars on the surface of the page aren't the only tools we rely on to achieve the focus. We rely, perhaps first of all, on the directions. We only attempt the effort because of the promise that the directions (and the offi-cial setting) hold forth. "Hey, reader!" it says. "There is something cool here for you to do. If you do it, here's what will happen. And now I'm going to tell you how to do it. Do just what I say, and you will get the cool result I promise."

Doing the Magic Eye means trusting the person who wrote the directions and the persons who published the puzzle. It means taking their word for it that this is a workable procedure that will issue in the result they promise. It means carefully trying to do exactly what their directions say, even when you don't know whether you're doing it right. It means allowing yourself to be taught how to see. Even as we must struggle to move through the surface particulars to an unknown beyond them, we must struggle to move through the words of the directions to an unknown beyond them. To do this takes trust and reliance—a kind of casting of ourselves on their mercy. If we were to withhold ourselves or suspend our judgment—if we were seriously to doubt the prospect—we'd never make the effort, and we'd never see the dolphins.

Yet another range of particulars on which we rely is the feelings in our body. We know these feelings in a lived way, from the inside. A hundred times an hour we adjust our optical focus length, just as when we're singing we can make our vocal chords match a hundred pitches, just as when we (well, some of us) are playing outfield we can catch a hundred differently placed line drives or long fly balls. We can do this with little conscious attention devoted to what our bodies do to make it happen. So when we come to follow these crazy direc-tions, it's our body that must follow them. Our body must embody them, crawl into them blindly, and then through them to an as yet unknown goal. And our body can do this, without our being able to put into words exactly what it is doing.

Surface details, body activity, and directions, then, represent three domains that we move through to access that on which we focus. The domains of subsidiaries are the world, our bodies, and the directions. The directions are the guiding words, the norms, the sense of the way things are.

And the *focus* itself, the goal of our act of knowing, is a coherent pattern, a unified and significant thing. We see . . . dolphins. We locate them beyond ourselves in the world. We see an entity with a coherent boundary, a three-dimensional figure that stands away from its background and away from us, with a front and sides and a hidden back side. It has meaning to us, a meaning the surface particulars didn't have. And our seeing it confirms that we've done the right thing to access it. We know we've reached what we were seeking. "Oh! I see it!" We can call it pattern-making, making sense of experience, connecting the dots.

So we have the particulars, now as subsidiaries embedded in the focus, we have the focal pattern or coherent whole, and we have our personal, sustained effort that vectors our grasp through the one to the other. This personal effort that shapes subsidiary particulars into a coherent focus can be called *integration*. It involves two kinds of awareness or attending: subsidiary awareness or attending *from* and focal awareness, or attending *to*. And the dynamic that connects through them is *me* (or *you*) in a very human and lively feat.

It's an act very much embedded in time. There is a time before we have first seen the dolphins (or any Magic Eye object). For some of us with the Magic Eye it is longer; for others, shorter. My kids take ten seconds. I take at least forty-five. My husband couldn't do it at all, until he got his first glasses. He was near-sighted in one eye and far-sighted in the other. You can't do the puzzles using only one eye. But the interesting thing here is this: We can and must begin to engage the particulars well before we can explicitly say what it is we are looking for. If we don't, we simply never find what we are looking for. The act of integration begins well before we are sure of the focus.

Once we have seen the dolphins, we continue to integrate from subsidiaries to maintain our grasp of the focus. We can lose sight of the dolphins and then have to struggle to regain it. What causes us to lose sight of the dolphins? Looking at the surface features of the page and no longer looking through them.

We can, with a book's worth of practice in the orthodontist's waiting room, build our skill and the speed with which we see the 3-D objects. We gradually learn to see what we're supposed to see. We still couldn't put into words what our eyes are doing, but we come to feel the rightness of it from the inside. Trusting the directions isn't such a big deal anymore because we have embodied them, because we know we're doing it right. And we hardly bother to think about the picture's surface anymore; we see dolphins.

It's interesting to note, by the way, that we call these *Magic* Eyes.

The Magic Eye is an act of knowing, and one that especially enables us to see the threefold structure of all epistemic acts. When we scrutinize other epistemic acts, we recognize this threefold structure—subsidiaries or clues, the focus we attend to through the subsidiaries, and the active and skilled human effort of integrating from the one to the other.

Think about recognizing a face. In a crowd of thousands in the mall at Christmas, you can pick out the face of your next-door neighbor. When you look at her face, you rely on innumerable particulars of her features to achieve the coherent pattern of her face. You don't reason from the particulars to her face. In fact, even if your life depended on it, you would have a hard time specifying all the particulars that you actually relied on to achieve your focus. Plus, she is always changing her hair color!

Think about lying in bed and hearing a strange noise. Suddenly your senses are straining to figure out what you heard, to make sense of your experience (to integrate to a focal pattern). Here's my story of a strange night noise—I'm sure you have one too, and you can think about it after you hear mine. Once when I was still a teenager living at home with my parents, I woke up to hear something that sounded like running water. My mind was straining for the answer. And my spine was tingling—was a burglar in the house? I crept slowly toward the sound. It was coming, it turned out, from the kitchen. The kitchen faucet was running, full tilt!

How could this be? Everybody was asleep in bed! Did the burglar have to wash his hands first? Then I recognized what must have happened. Our faucet worked by a single handle/stick that you pulled forward. What I found was a large zucchini squash from my father's garden wedged behind that handle! I surmised that it must have rolled off the windowsill where my mother had put it for further ripening. And I surmised that a puff of summer breeze through the screen had been the culprit.

Can you see that for a few moments there I was struggling to integrate some puzzling particulars into a sensible pattern? When I accomplished this, I felt I knew what had happened. I had made sense of my initially bewildering experience.

When we understand the facets of the act of knowing, we can see readily how knowing has the same structure as any human skill. Consider any skill you may have: shooting baskets, playing a musical composition on the piano, knitting a sweater, driving a car, hammering a nail, breast-feeding a baby, or riding a bike. In each of these you rely on body experiences to focus on the activity. In order to develop the skill, your body had to learn the experiences. It had to learn to carry them out and to recognize what it felt like to carry them out. You had to develop a felt sense, or a body sense. You probably learned this under the guidance of a teacher or coach, who told you what to look for and how important it is, and who looked at what you were doing to give you feedback about whether you are doing it right. When you began to learn the skill, you probably struggled to get it right and to know that you got it right. You focused on the body experiences. Now that you are good at the skill, you don't focus on the body experiences. You rely on the body experiences, focusing through them on the skilled achievement. I hung up a poster in the basement today, hammering pins through it into the wall. I never thought about the hammer. I really only thought about getting the poster up on the wall.

When you are good at the skill, if you stop and focus back on the body experiences, whatever you are doing is liable to come to a crashing halt. Try thinking about your fingers in the middle of your piano recital. The same thing happens with the Magic Eye picture. If your eyes focus back on the plane of the picture, the dolphins disappear. This shows that we are aware of the particulars in a fundamentally different way from the way we are aware of the focus. We can distinguish subsidiary awareness from focal awareness. And the relationship between the two is asymmetrical. When you try to treat the subsidiaries as a focus you destroy, in that effort, the epistemic act in question.

So what goes on in human knowing? What does it mean to know? Coming to know involves actively struggling to rely on a collection of as yet unrelated particulars to achieve a focus on a coherent pattern or whole. This subsidiary-focal integrative structure characterizes all significantly human acts. *The act of knowing is the human's skilled coping with the world through achieving a coherence, an integrated pattern, a making sense of things, that opens the world to us.* That's a mouthful; we'll be chewing it slowly in the next several chapters.

For Further Thought and Discussion

Define the terms. Look back over the chapter for definitions of these terms. It will help you as you read farther to get a handle on them:

- Focus
- Subsidiaries

Surface features

Body clues

Directions

• Integration

Identify other "Oh! I see it!" moments. Name some other experiences you have had when you felt as if you moved from not knowing something to knowing it. Sometimes we call these light bulb experiences. Compare these experiences to the Magic Eye and to each other. Do they have similar features?

Identify a skill. Name the skill at which you think you are best.

• Can you find the same features present in this skill?
    When did you feel as if you "got it"?
    What do you focus on when you perform the skill?
    What do you rely on when you perform the skill?
    Did you have a coach when learning the skill?
• How did you feel about the activity before you learned the skill?
• What were key factors in your gaining the skill?
• Does the skill make you feel more or less in touch with the world?

Draw some conclusions about knowing.

• How plausible does it seem to you to say that what we observe in the Magic Eye experience characterizes every act of knowing? Why?
• Can you think of other experiences you would call acts of knowing that did not involve you in "Oh! I see it!" moments?
• How does this model help you to understand what is involved in knowing?

Consider knowing God. Do you see things in your experience of God that this model explains?

PART II

. . . Is the Responsible Human Struggle . . .

Knowing
is the responsible human struggle
to rely on clues
to focus on a coherent pattern
and submit to its reality.

7

Laying Out for a Frisbee

The Knower's Risky, Responsible Struggling

As my daughters have become teenagers, I have learned new lingo from them and their friends. I also pick up some things from my students. One of my new phrases is "laying out." One Sunday afternoon, the lunch crowd at my house headed out to the cul-de-sac for a game of Frisbee. A couple of young men admired my efforts: "Wooo! She's laying out!" Okay, I didn't exactly slide head-first across the concrete. They were being teasingly generous. But I went to class next time with a fresh metaphor for the act of knowing.

The dimensions of human knowing that we learned to see as we talked about the Magic Eye are so important to understand, not to mention so exciting and valuable to grasp, that I want to linger with them. Learning to think about knowing in this way is the key to hope when it comes to our main question—whether we can know God. It offers hope about whether we can know anything at all. It dissolves some of the puzzles about knowing that have plagued thinkers for centuries, puzzles generated by a faulty, unrealistic model of knowing. And it helps us see things in fresh and exciting ways, for it aptly and evocatively fits our ordinary human experience. We're no longer wearing an epistemological straitjacket; we're wearing an epistemological leotard.

It's important that we linger with this model of knowing so as to learn it. Have you seen yet that we're *knowing* knowing? *Learning about* learning? One very fun feature about talking about knowing is that you are unavoidably engaged in the very act of doing what you are talking about! Talk about immediate application of what you are learning!

So if this model of knowing is new to you, then here is what is going on as you read this book. The words in this book and the experiences of your world are like the surface details of the Magic Eye. You are struggling to make sense of your life and of my words. I, also by way of these words, am a coach giving directions, suggesting how to make sense of things, holding forth the hope of what that "sense" will look like, teaching you how to see, and giving you opportunities to practice your skill. If I were with you in person, I would also be able to give you feedback about how you're doing: "Now you're getting it!" Or "No, that's not quite right," and so on. But whether I am alongside you in person or in the words of this book, in order for you to learn, I must offer myself and my thoughts in my words, and you must struggle to get inside my words, or get my words inside you and figure out from the inside what they mean.

Human knowing, we said, involves actively struggling to rely on a collection of as yet unrelated particulars to achieve a focus on a coherent pattern or whole. It is a skilled coping with the world through achieving a coherence, an integrated pattern, a making sense of things, that opens the world to us. We identified a three-fold structure: the clues, the struggle, and the focus. In this section I want to talk more about the struggle—the knower's active struggle to integrate the clues into a focus. That active struggle is a little like laying out for a frisbee.

■ The Personal Claim That Makes a Claim a Claim

On the modernist model of knowledge, if the default mode in my brain is to be believed, we identified knowledge with informative statements that are true. When I say "knowledge," you may think of stated facts, like "2 + 2 = 4," or "The first president of the United States of America was George Washington," or "Tiger Woods is a great golfer," or "My car needs a new power steering pump." We tend to think of these as out there, floating around unattached, like so many asteroids.

Conceiving of knowledge in this way blinds us to some things we need to see for knowledge to make any sense. We need to see that our truth claims grow out of and are upheld by humans in a very human effort. I think this effort that spawns and never stops undergirding our claims deserves to be included as a component in what we call knowledge. That's why I prefer to talk about human acts of knowing, as opposed to knowledge. Knowing involves statements, but it doesn't mistakenly divorce those statements from the knower who is affirming them.

Let's talk, for example, about the statement "My car needs a new power steering pump." What I wrote on the page just now is not my knowing of it, though of course it artificially expresses my knowing act. My knowing of it, my holding it as true, is more like a credo, my professing my commitment to its truth. It's like my signing a check, or my saying, "I do." I assert it. We sometimes talk about putting our necks on the line. We do this with every claim we assert.

I'm telling you: My car needs a new power steering pump. My assertion has its roots in the tingling alarm that spreads over my body as the car's steering wheel resists my attempts to turn it. My body sense is further shaped and informed by my mechanic's over-the-phone diagnosis. I embody my claim; it propels me to action. I make a beeline for his gas station, anxiously tugging at the wheel every step of the way. My actions lead eventually to my being restored bodily to the world: after the repair I take the curves of a park-side road with delight, windows open, radio pumping road music.

If a statement is a dot, the act of knowing is a vector to and through the dot. It's like laying out for a frisbee. It has a point of origin in my embodied and world-situated being. It takes a direction from me, through my effort to orchestrate and rely on features of my experience whose relevance and even existence I cannot fully validate or articulate, to and then through a focal pattern to the world beyond. Through that focus I unlock and evoke a world.

All of this active human effort characterizes every act of human knowing. It is true of it the first time we come to know something. It is also required to maintain through time that some claim is true. Once you come to understand that something is true, it is still *you* who are affirming that it is true. It takes an ongoing personal affirmation.

▊ All Truth Is Somebody's Truth

What does it mean to say that a statement is true? *My car needs a new power steering pump.* If I know this, I am holding it to be true. Truth is always somebody's truth, in the sense that a truth claim is a truth claimed, a truth that somebody claims or asserts. A truth claim "unclaimed" doesn't even count as a candidate for knowledge. But that is the trivial fact. Once you see it, it's obvious, but it doesn't say much.

Many people today have come to realize that all truth is somebody's truth. Misguided as we have been by the faulty modernist model of knowing, we found it unsettling to admit the reality of what seemed, in contrast to the objective ideal we sought, a subjective defect in the process. It was upsetting to admit to ourselves that people disagree about what the truth is, and to acknowledge that what people think is true is shaped in a telling way by what they've experienced and by what they want. This subjective component is just the thing that the modernist model of knowing has called us to eliminate in the name of objectivity in knowledge.

We've gradually come to admit that we can't eliminate it. But we have mistakenly concluded that admitting it would be the death of truth. The moment we acknowledged this personal component, we thought it meant the end to knowledge. We thought we were left with relativism (everybody makes up his or her own truth) or skepticism (there ain't no truth). But really, all truth has been somebody's truth as long as there have been persons to know truth. It was as true for modernists such as Descartes (even though they didn't see it) as it is for postmodernists such as Richard Rorty.

You may have been frightened by this prospect, too, as have I. But it isn't the end of truth or knowledge. It is, quite literally, the beginning. Our misconceptions concerning knowing and objectivity kept us from recognizing both the trivial fact that all truth is somebody's truth as well as the more substantial one about laying out.

■ Personally Engaging the World through Our Claims

The trivial fact has a positive and profound counterpart: The act of knowing actively involves the human agent. All stated facts, even $2 + 2 = 4$, crest an unstatable active human effort much as a skin crusts a cooling cup of hot chocolate. Like so many shining electrical bulbs, truth claims tap into a current without which they would not be what they are.

Truth is not rendered arbitrary and relative by my involvement. It is embedded and actualized in my involvement. It is connected to me; it lives in my engaging. It is formally unstatable, but not because it is irrational; it is unstatable because I am living it. I live in $2 + 2 = 4$, when I affirm it, the way I live in the hammer I used to hang the poster. I don't just stand there and look at it. Or if I do, it isn't knowledge, even as looking at the hammer isn't going to get the poster on the wall. Without the knower's sustained and committed effort of relying on clues in search of a focus, it just isn't an act of knowing, and knowing just doesn't happen.

Statements of truth express and extend my disposing of myself in the world. They pull me beyond myself to meet a world that they also unlock to meet me. They can say more than I think they say, letting in a world that transforms my words. If you restrict knowledge to the sentence lying on the page, it makes no sense, for it is a fish out of water. It has within it no shred of power to make it true or false. It's like a hammer lying on a table, untouched by human hands and power. We often don't notice this because we rightly connect a hammer with both our past exploits as builders and a host of future possibilities. But the hammer only makes sense, it only engages the world truthfully, in our hands. The act of knowing is the laying out of ourselves through a claim to engage the world.

■ Risky Responsibility

Picking out a pattern involves us not only in a struggle but also in responsible personal initiative, choice, and assessment, and a measure of risk. It takes a personal assessment to *notice* anything. When my steering wheel resists my touch, I am the one who notices it, who sizes up the degree of resistance and judges that it exceeds some unspecified level of propriety for cars with power steering. It may actually be something more visceral and less cerebral than a statement, for the "noticing" begins in my fingertips. For all that, it is no less I, no less a personal, evaluative act. It is I who choose to trust my mechanic's diagnosis and to respond to his "Bring it in." I could be wrong. I may get to the shop, in fear and trembling, only to be told it was in my head (so to speak). Or maybe the problem is far worse. As I risk the trip to the shop (rather than pay a tow truck), I may lose complete control of the car, resulting in consequences I do not even wish to postulate. My statement, "My car needs a new power steering pump," verbalizes the personal commitment that comes to expression in my action. I exercise responsibility, and I incur risk.

The act of knowing is a risky disposing of our beings, a passionate commitment to trust things we cannot fully justify at the time of our effort. Just as the person who truly lays out for a Frisbee risks crashing to the ground, with or without the Frisbee.

It is highly appropriate to apply words such as commitment, passion, longing, love, and faith to this manner of disposing ourselves which is the epistemic

59

act. As I come to understand the theory of relativity, I move myself out into its statements and through them into the world. I lay out for them as those guys do for a Frisbee. This is commitment, love, and faith. But it is not subjectivistic, relativistic, privatistic—those unfortunate labels that many have thrown at faith and that many have embraced as the death of truth. It is not subjectivistic; it is human. It is embodied, responsible human skill.

It's like Tiger Woods wielding a 9-iron. We're not tempted to call that subjectivistic, or privatistic, or anything short of awesome. In his swing we see the human body at a peak of excellence, solidly, brilliantly engaging the world. It is a beautifully active human effort. It gives a whole new meaning to the word *commitment!* So did Einstein's saying $E = mc^2$. Knowing, holding a claim to be true, is an awesome, active, human effort.

■ Knowing Auto Mechanics and God: Vectoring through My Claims to Engage the World

When I say that my auto mechanic is good and reliable, I am claiming that that statement is true. I cannot affirm it without affirming it (duh!). In saying it, I commit myself to its truth. It is my truth, but in saying it, I offer it simply as truth.

It is a laying out of myself. It originates in experiences I have described to you. It moves from them through layers of my being. I rely on clues within and outside of me, and others' words of recommendation, as I focus on Jeff's reputation. I dispose myself, perhaps riskily, in holding to the claim. I might be wrong. My trust may prove to have been misplaced. You may think poorly of me as you drive to another mechanic. But I persevere in the claim, not because I am entitled to personal preference in a private truth, but because I think I'm right. The claim shapes my behavior. I trust him with my car. I keep trusting myself to my car. I lay out through the claim to grasp and engage the real. I navigate the streets of St. Louis with joy and confidence for the future because he is there.

To be a Christian involves claiming that the God of the Bible exists and is like it describes him. It involves claiming that this is true. I cannot affirm it without affirming it. In saying it, I commit myself to its truth. It is my truth, in this respect, but in saying it, I offer it simply as truth.

It is a laying out of myself. It originates in an array of my experiences. It moves from them through layers of my being. I rely on, live in, clues within and outside of me, others' words of recommendation, and what I take to be the authoritative word of Scripture, as I focus on God. I dispose myself, perhaps riskily, in holding to the claim. I might be wrong. My trust may prove to have been misplaced. You may think poorly of me. But I persevere in the claim, not because I am entitled to personal preference in a private truth, but because I think I'm right.

The claim shapes my behavior. I believe that God is Lord of the universe. I live out this belief in my effort to do what he says and love what he loves. I look to him for the unconditional love and protection that I cannot guarantee myself and do not deserve. I lay out through the claim, and through it I grasp and engage the real. I know his world in light of its maker and redeemer. And I sense the joy of engaging the world more profoundly, in a way that shapes my past and floods me with wild prospects for the future. Thus, the act of knowing God shares with the act of knowing an auto mechanic this central vector of human commitment.

For Further Thought and Discussion

Find your own examples. What are some things that you do in which your body vectors outward, like the Frisbee player's does? Or what are some such wonderful moments you have observed?

Draw your own comparison to your truth claims.

- Give a couple of examples of your own truth claims.
- Align those claims in your mind with the moment when the Frisbee player grabs the Frisbee, or whatever the corresponding moment is in your own example.
- Identify your actual asserting of the claim, your effort first to appropriate it (learn it, discover it), and your activity that expresses your holding it true, by aligning these with the laying out vector that passes through the Frisbee grab.
- Does the idea of vectoring provide an apt metaphor for your claiming something to be true? In what ways? How or in what ways does it not?

Consider the nature of knowing. How does this metaphor revise your conception of knowing in general? How does that revision affect what you think about knowing God?

8

Lewis and Clark Did It Best

Acts of Coming to Know—the Paradigm of Knowing, Rather than the Exception

Seeing that knowing is at its heart an active human achievement helps us reconnect some things torn from each other by a misguided model of how we know. One is reconnecting discovery to knowledge. The old model of knowledge, overlooking as it did the human effort that makes knowing what it is, couldn't figure out what to do with discovery and learning. How can discovery be knowledge? How do you get from not knowing to knowing?

A mistaken view of knowledge as statements "floating" independently of ourselves masks not only the knower's ongoing affirmative effort. It also is a view we can hold only if we forget or minimize the effort that went into achieving that knowledge the first time around. We forget what it took to learn some of our commonplace truths.

I taught our three daughters the basics of reading and writing and arithmetic. I will never forget my surprise when teaching the first one, Starr, her numbers: she had to learn the numeral 7. She could say her numbers, 1 to 10 and beyond. She could count objects. She could say "seven," and she could write 7. But she didn't know and had to learn that 7, the mark on the page, stood for the concept of "seven"! Now, at seventeen, having moved through arithmetic, algebra, geometry, trigonometry, and analysis, Starr only knows of her early effort when I tell her the story. But she relies all the time on 7 meaning the concept "seven."

▮ How Can You Come to Know Anything at All?

The old understanding of knowledge as depersonalized, disembodied pieces of information, explainable only by reference to other depersonalized pieces of information, found it difficult to explain the way we come to know the first time around. It stuck to explaining what it did know, which was how to explain one piece of information in reference to other known pieces of information. Acts of coming to know were often dismissed as something not really involving knowledge so much as luck or creativity.

It's fine to say that acts of coming to know involve luck or creativity; it's not fine to say that they are not knowledge. If a key kind of knowing doesn't fit our model, it's not right to discredit the knowing; it's right to discredit the model. This reminds me of the joke about the inebriated man whom the police officer encounters searching the ground in the pool of light under a streetlight. He reports that he is searching for his keys. When asked where he lost them, the man responds that he doesn't know, but he can only search where there is light! This is what we do when we so define knowledge that discovery no longer makes any sense.

I'm sure you've learned what is commonly called the "scientific method." In my daughter Stephanie's seventh-grade classroom last year, the scientific method was printed on a gargantuan, laminated poster on the bulletin board: Find a problem; collect data; form a tentative hypothesis to explain the data; test the hypothesis; draw a conclusion. Nobody seems to want to talk about how you form a tentative hypothesis.

The textbook I use to teach critical thinking devotes a section to scientific reasoning. It tells you how to reason to a conclusion once you have generated a hypothesis. It tells you nothing about how to generate a hypothesis. All it says concerning hypothesis generation is this: "A hypothesis is a free creation of the mind used to structure the evidence and unveil the pattern that lies beneath the surface." This I believe is an accurate and telling statement. The author also affirms accurately that the hypothesis also directs the search for evidence. But this is all that is said.

I think I faced this difficulty when I was in high school and thinking I would go on to study chemistry in college. I was, frankly, hesitant about the prospect. Part of my hesitation was epistemological. I remember thinking: running three tests in lab to prove a principle discovered a hundred years ago won't make me into a discoverer in the field of chemistry. I couldn't see how a person comes to know.

I thought the same way about playing the piano, incidentally. I listened (as did everybody else) to my immensely talented older sister play the piano. She was even my teacher. But I couldn't see how I could ever get from what my fingers did to what her fingers did with any amount of practice. I didn't even trust that my sister could teach me. It was partly an epistemic problem. I focused on particulars that apparently bore no relation to the intended coherent outcome. I saw no way to reason from one to the other. I was a child of the Western philosophy, and on the skeptical end of the scale.

Meno, Socrates' student in Plato's dialogue by that name, expressed my epistemic problem well. Meno asked Socrates, "How will you look for something when you don't in the least know what it is?" Socrates restated his dilemma: "A man cannot try to discover either what he knows or what he does not know. He would not seek what he knows, for since he knows it there is no need of the inquiry, nor what he does not know, for in that case he does not even know what he is to look for." If you restrict knowledge to that which you can put into words, your model of knowledge doesn't offer any help concerning how to get off the starting block or out of the gate.

■ The Recipe for Discovery

If knowledge is "just the facts, ma'am," then there is no knowledge, because there is no arriving at it. Knowledge, in its first achieving and in its everyday assertion, crests an active human effort. This creative and active human effort is overlooked and impossible to explain when we restrict knowledge to its articulable aspects. Knowledge is the statement, the words that say something. If that's all there is to knowledge, then the discoverer or the learner, if he or she is honest, must side with the romanticists and with Plotinus: What is most important in life, and even in knowledge, is not knowledge.

This skeptical child, anyway, needed to know that the magic of her sister's playing was ordinary though awesome human skill that lies at the heart of any knowing. I needed to know that nobody gets from point A to point B, even in a deductive syllogism, apart from human effort, and that with that effort, things that border on miraculous are part of everyday human life. The human knower in fact is able, through persistent and passionate commitment, relying on skill, and guided by a hard-to-specify sense of how things are, to achieve coherent patterns that grasp an aspect of reality.

I needed to know that this happens because, in the act of coming to know, the knower-to-be relies on sensed but as yet inarticulable clues. At the time he or she uses them as clues, he or she is not yet able to put into words what the clues are. And I needed to be told to accredit this intuitive (not mystical, but human and skilled) aptitude. All epistemic achievements come in time through the hard-to-put-into-words but very human shaping of more-than-could-be-put-into-words features of our lives. The knower does this at first stumblingly and then, with experience, skillfully.

It's not that "Formulate tentative hypotheses" is undoable; it's that all acts of knowing—the selecting a problem, the collecting the data, the testing the hypotheses, and the drawing conclusions—are equally rooted in skilled human effort. What the modern model of knowing refused to admit was the existence and necessity of knowing that can't be put into words. And in so doing, it missed the lived feel of the thing.

In fact practicing test runs in the high school lab is a valuable exercise that builds a future scientist's skill. In fact the grade schooler's keyboard scales help build a skill that she eventually employs in playing Gershwin's *Rhapsody in Blue*. The practice prompts sound integrations. Science teachers and piano teachers in fact do say helpful things and assign helpful projects. By submitting to their guidance we can in fact become scientists and pianists. But the things they say, we should recognize, are maxims that guide the student to develop a skill. They are not facts from which a conclusion is deduced. Speaking the facts doesn't lead to the goal; embodying the facts does. Then we haven't got a rational deduction. But we do end up with a discovery. This is why learning and discovery have moved forward despite our failure to appreciate and represent accurately what it was we were doing.

■ First Acts Reveal Key Features of Knowing

Welcoming first acts of knowing back into the epistemological fold helps us to see the act of knowing in fresh and helpful ways. It is our first attempt at the Magic Eye that especially helps us identify the three-fold structure present every time we look at the book in the orthodontist's waiting room. It gives us a better grasp of what goes into the act of knowing.

And acts of coming to know are rightly deemed the more exciting and heroic. Their risk and courage deserve to be celebrated. They make documentaries about Lewis and Clark getting to the West Coast, not about my getting to the

West Coast. What a feat of knowing a scientific discovery is! What a feat it was when you learned to use the Pythagorean theorem!

Thinking about discoveries and learning helps us to see that an act of knowing often spans a period of time. It could be seconds, hours, days, months, years. When I thought of knowledge in the old way, knowledge didn't seem to have anything to do with time. It was timeless. But, in fact, there was a time before you even had any connection with what you were coming to know, then a time when the puzzle came to life, then a period of time when you were fighting your way to understanding, then a time when you figured it out, then a time when you moved beyond that focus to yet another.

The human aptitude for integration, operating as it does before its first achievement, includes foreknowing, an anticipative knowing. We know this experience well in our ordinary life. Someone says to you—"See that guy over there? What's his name?" You say, "Oh! I can't remember! But give me a minute—" and then you start to rack your brain in search of . . . what? After a time you say the most amazing thing: "It's on the tip of my tongue!" And then, you have it! We have a sense of getting closer to the solution.

All this helps us see that when it comes to knowing, there are key portions of the whole thing that cannot be expressed in words. If there is a "before" to our knowing, then there is a kind of knowing going on that can't be represented verbatim in the description of the thing we have yet to come to know. You can't call it "not knowing," either, by the way. But if we didn't consider those portions part of the knowing, knowledge, and especially coming to knowledge, would devolve into absurdity.

Acts of discovery, acts of learning, acts of critical verification or affirmation, and acts of conversion are all acts of coming to know. Lewis and Clark seeking a way to the Pacific, a cook figuring out how to make the best chocolate chip cookies, a scientist taking a stand on the reality of a significant numerical correlation, a school board hiring a new high school principal, coming to embrace a fresh political policy or philosophical stance—these are so many epistemic acts in process. We may not be Lewis or Clark, but we continually learn, extending our horizons and our insight. It may be math class, or it may be parenting a teenager, learning to crochet, or figuring out where your spouse happens to be at the moment. In each case we navigate in light of indications that we are unable, at the time that we rely on them, to specify fully. Yet our very human aptitude for this, and our human longing for the truth, enable us skillfully, though never flawlessly, to move forward.

■ Coming to Know Auto Mechanics and God

Choosing an auto mechanic, determining to rely on him, is an act of coming to know. There is no way that, before your first visit to the garage, you will have firsthand or exhaustive information. You have, perhaps as I did, a word of recommendation from a person or persons you are only just getting to know. You take a first plunge, and find your confidence borne out in a well-timed motor, tightened brakes, and an updated oil change sticker. Or perhaps you don't know this mechanic from Adam, and you pick his name out of a phone book at a pay phone in a moment of emergency. You don't know him; you just know you need help, and his ad in the yellow pages touts his qualifications. You gradually build your sense of the auto mechanic's skills and business practices out of contacts over time. Mine will pick up my car from the seminary; but you have to leave the key under the mat. I can tell the car's been test-driven when I find the radio on a strange station. You navigate by hinted possibilities concerning horizons of his capacities: here's a guy I perhaps could trust to advise me if I were buying a used car. Here's a guy who will dispose properly of the car's replaced oil. Wow—here's a guy who pumps gasoline for his mother's car. That's got some sort of significance! Maybe it has to do with honoring moms; he's got a sense of respect. I can expect him to treat me respectfully, too. You move from unknowing to knowing. Each car problem or inspection offers another opportunity to determine to rely on him.

Coming to know God is like this. You hear a friend describe what the Bible says about God and about why you need to know him. It makes surprising and humbling sense of your experience. It makes sense of your significance and glory; it makes sense of your brokenness. It holds the prospect of being the very thing you've been longing for. You decide to take the risk and reach out to Jesus Christ, asking him to forgive your rebellion and trusting him to save you.

For some people, conversion is a long time coming. For others many things fall in to place suddenly. It may feel like a risky critical affirmation or a no-brainer acclamation.

For anyone coming to know God, it is a process that extends from before the initial act of trust through each day of the rest of life. Our act of knowing God, the Bible indicates, will only reach fruition when Jesus returns. In our knowing him now, we live with a lot of not-yet knowing. The apostles in their letters regularly pray for their disciples "that you may know him better." Our study of the Bible, combined with our experiences of our selves and our world over time, builds our grasp of who God is. We grow in knowing him as we try to do what he says to do. So it is that knowing God, like knowing an auto mechanic, involves a moving from unknowing to knowing, and at each point of contact fresh decisions to trust and follow are called for.

For Further Thought and Discussion

Find your own examples. Name some things that you can remember learning or discovering or coming to know. Choose one of these to think about more deeply. Describe your experience.

- Can you remember a time before you knew you needed to know that thing?
- Can you remember a time when you knew you needed to know it but didn't yet know what you needed to know?
- What prompted this hard-to-define awareness?
- Later, did you have a sense of getting closer to knowing the answer?
- After having learned the answer, could you look back and recognize clues that had guided you to your discovery?
- Can you remember how those clues appeared to you before you learned the answer?

Consider the nature of knowing. How does thinking about coming to know affect your conception of knowing in general?

Consider coming to know God. Locate yourself on a continuum of coming to know God. In which area do you think you are at the moment?

- I don't think that there is anything there for me to know.
- There are things in my experience that prompt me to wonder about whether there is a God.
- I'm pursuing knowing God, and I feel a sense of getting closer.
- I've already come to know God, but I keep struggling to know him better.
- I thought I had come to know God, but I feel as if I've lost sight of the pattern.

9

The Struggle
That Makes Us Human

Longing to Know–Irresistible
and Essentially Human

The act of knowing continually vectors us outward. It moves from us, outward to a focus, and beyond. The clues on which we rely are always near us; we indwell them. The pattern we seek to achieve is always a bit beyond us. We orient ourselves toward that which we seek.

What's more, although achieving a coherence is a satisfying end point of the struggle at hand, we always in time reach through it, interiorize it in search of further coherences. You probably didn't quit math once you had learned the Pythagorean theorem! Nor did Starr quit when she figured out that 7 meant "seven." After a certain coherence is first achieved, we advance to rely on it— it joins other subsidiary clues—in our search for further coherences.

As a result, we can see ourselves as a layering up of skilled coherences. You are a center, extending through and indwelling your developed skills and capacities. You advance through the skills to regions beyond. Your being holds promise of future possibilities.

First we learned our alphabet and the use of a pencil; then we learned words and how to read and write; now we rely on these critical skills subsidiarily to focus far beyond them—at the moment, on profound questions about knowing and about God. In fact, the fact that we long to know ultimate reality aptly expresses the continually outward movement of our knowing.

Catching Frisbees, so to speak, proves irresistible! Humans "lay out," struggle to know. Humans fight to make sense of their experience! How many times in our day and in our lives do we do this! Your roommate is acting uncharacteristically; you immediately begin to search for an explanation. Or your roses are failing to bloom. Or you take a new class in a new subject with a new professor, and you find yourself immersed in terminology about as transparent as so many pieces of granite. You fight to make sense of what he or she is saying. Or your parents divorce, and you ask yourself desperately, What happened? What does this say about me? What does it say about them? What does it say about God?

Trying to make sense of experiences is somewhat of a compulsion for humans. One day when our children were smaller, together we pieced together a 100-piece jigsaw puzzle. In the process, we came upon a piece that I recognized belonged in a different puzzle. I set it to the side. A couple of days later I gave the piece to my daughter, Stacey. "Please take this downstairs and put it in the box it belongs in," I asked her. It occurred to me to wonder to myself, "Will she be able to resist getting the puzzle out and doing it?" A short time later, I walked by the den. There she was with all the pieces arrayed on the floor, and the puzzle half assembled! She couldn't resist doing the puzzle!

Now, maybe you can resist a 100-piece jigsaw puzzle. But there are any number of other puzzles, achievements, and attempts at coherence that you have not been able to resist. Try to think of some. As you think of your own efforts, do you not see that among them are the acts that are you at your most human, and the acts by which, as a human, you engage the world? Struggling for coherence is the profoundly human act of engaging the world. And, it is knowing.

■ Caring, Coping

Why do we struggle to achieve coherence? The answer may sound lame because it is so basic: struggling for coherence is part and parcel of being human. In Continental philosopher Martin Heidegger's words, *Dasein,* the uniquely human experience, is intrinsically *caring* and *coping.* It is arguable that if we no longer care about making sense of things, no longer cope with our affairs, we are very sick or not far from death.

Have you ever been sick enough not to care about anything at all? When can you tell that you are getting better? Isn't when you start to care about things that need doing? To be a healthy human is to be compelled to integrate, to make sense of experience. Even in the task at hand, thinking about if and how we know God, we search for a coherence that makes sense of our experience. The best readers of this book will be the ones passionately struggling to make sense of the prospect of knowing God. Apart from some desire to make sense of your experience, you probably would not have reached this point in the book! Your longing sustains your effort.

To be human is to make sense of experience, to develop our world and extend our influence even as we extend our conceptual grasp.

Here's one of the things about the God of the Bible that fits so well with this aspect of knowing that it confirms to me his believability. In the Bible's story of creation, God made the humans and then gave them a defining command (and I paraphrase): "Image me by extending my rule, by caring for and developing my world." He commands humans to represent him within his creation by continuing to develop it and care for it in ways that will bless it. In my opinion, he had already made humans in such a way that they couldn't resist the sense-making to which he summoned them! What I find is that we humans have been given a built-in compulsion to develop creation by making sense of it. We as humans are compulsive carers. Human acts of knowing are care-born integrations by which we extend ourselves into the world, shaping and developing the world as we go.

We can't not fulfill the command! We can, however, do it well or do it poorly. Humans will never perfectly blend in with the nonhuman environment. Their glory is to shape it. But will it issue in blessing or curse for creation? Walt Disney's *Lion King* graphically illustrates the curse of bad rule and the blessing of responsible rule: Scar's domain is scorched and lifeless, with hungry and broken inhabitants; Simba's, once he has embraced his responsibility, is full of color and life and joyful inhabitants. Disney confirms what Scripture says about the blessing of just and righteous rule. Our integrated patterns shape the world even as we access it by means of them. In our passion to connect the dots, we fulfill our calling as humans, and we confirm what the Bible says about God.

To be human is to make sense of experience. There are voices today that would discourage the attempt. They say, You can't really get it right, you can't really understand. All you can do is come up with some private interpretation, and you need not worry about your private interpretation fitting the world, because there is no world for it to fit. And for you to think you can get it right, objectively right, is an attitude that threatens everyone else's freedom to think what they like. It is socially inappropriate to believe you can understand, or make sense of experience, in any objective way. It is socially inappropriate to long to know. So keep your opinions in the realm of the private, please.

Not to make sense of experience is, however, not to be human. What I want to say is this: Don't let these antagonistic voices win the day! Do not deny or repress your own fundamentally human passion to make sense of experience. As a human, I believe, *you long to know.* Do not surrender the passion. And as you pursue understanding, have the courage to admit both that your conclusions might be wrong, and that you also believe you are right. But don't give up the pursuit. Don't let yourself believe that it is inappropriate. In reality, we engage in the struggle to connect the dots throughout huge portions of our experience, whether we acknowledge this penchant or not. This is only a call to authenticity—honest admission of what is already going on. Humans make sense of experience. In this way they navigate life and give expression to their longings. Don't stop loving the longing.

■ Knowing and Doing

The traditional model of knowledge that we have inherited from the Greeks, that extends through millennia down to us, typically divorces knowing from doing. It is possible to think about something in abstraction from acting on it. While there are times in our experience when it is useful to make this distinction, the distinction has the adverse effect of leading us to think of action as mindless and mind as actionless. Knowledge, we are led to say, is to be had even if it does not shape our behavior.

But we all know that in many circumstances of life, not to act in a certain situation is quite simply not to have understood. Suppose you run into my office and shout at me—"There's a fire in the basement!" Suppose I reply, "That's nice," and keep writing. Would you say that I understood what you were saying? I think not.

On the other hand, we have tended to overlook the epistemic component of action. You have probably heard me say that all significant human acts may very well be acts of knowing. Wordless acts nevertheless affirm truth claims. That's how it is that someone can show you that he or she cares about you by sending you flowers, inviting you into his or her home, silently stroking your shoulder as you cry.

Did you see the movie *Cool Runnings,* about the bobsled team from Jamaica? I remember that one of the team members wanted to achieve his Olympic dream because he wanted to live in a palace that looked like a picture on a postcard he carried around with him. When the going got rough at one point, he tore up the picture. At another point in the story, one of the other team members retrieved the postcard bits from the trash, put them back together, and silently gave the card back to its owner. The first man's action said, "My dream is unattainable. I am worthless." The second man in his action countered these claims: "Your dream is attainable, and you are significant."

Knowing is, at its heart, an act. To act is to live, embody, knowledge. The act of knowing is a profoundly human one. And it is a struggle toward coherence.

▮ Knowing Auto Mechanics and God: A Profoundly Human Longing to Know

I feel compelled to orchestrate the shreds of my experience with my auto mechanic into a coherent and meaningful whole: Jeff is a good and reliable auto mechanic. I may say this to you. Or I may, simply, repeatedly take my car to him and act on what he says. Were you to observe my action over time, you would very well articulate it using the same description.

You and I both, in our words and resoundingly in our action, make statements about God. All humans worship . . . something. I could tell, as I knew you better, what or who your God is by considering the joint meaning of your actions. In fact, I'd like to suggest, worship is the epistemic act of making sense of the whole of our lives. And we as humans are compelled inwardly to do it.

We're used to saying, "Actions speak louder than words." And we know this is true, for good or for ill. By the same token, people who know the God of the Bible live their knowledge by trying to do what he says, orienting their lives to his reality and lordship. We're all pretty sensitive to inconsistencies when we consider religious people. We label it hypocrisy. It's not a very nice reality.

To draw this out a little further: I think we all know that humans are either enriched or cheapened by their choice of what they worship. We know what it is to have "noble ideals." We know what it is to "put something on a pedestal" that doesn't really belong there. The former makes us more the humans we are meant to be. The latter cheapens us.

I think that this is just the point of the first and second of the Ten Commandments: "No other gods but me"; "No idols." There is, the Bible indicates, no created reality that we can idolize and thereby become more human. Instead, in the idolizing, we are dehumanized, and we are less ourselves. We can only become more human, more ourselves, when we worship not the creature, but the Creator.

Whatever we worship, it is an orientation that shapes our lives, that comes to expression in our action. And it is a struggle to integrate from every corner of our experience to a coherent pattern.

Yes, knowing God is a pattern making that draws together every aspect of our lives. Knowing an auto mechanic is a pattern that encompasses a range of far smaller proportions. But knowing God, when it comes to embodying a struggle for a coherent pattern, is no different in kind from knowing your auto mechanic.

For Further Thought and Discussion

Find your own examples.

- Give examples of your own longings to know, to connect the dots, to make sense of experience.
- Have there been voices in your experience discouraging you from embracing the longing to know?
- Which of these, your efforts to make sense of experience or your denying this passion, make you more yourself, more human?

Consider your life.

- Whom or what do you worship? In responding to this question, try to take into consideration not only your explicit thoughts but also what your actions would also speak. You may find it helpful to substitute the question, Whom or what would my best friend or my family say that I worship? Or you could ask them!
- How is your object of worship a pattern that connects the dots for you, to which your life as a whole is one big integrative struggle?
- How does thinking about these questions affect what you think about coming to know God?
- Could it be said that our human longing to make sense of experience is at its very bottom a longing to know him?

10

Integration, Not Deduction

The Knowing Process: Transformational, Rather than Linear

The human effort that links clues to focus and beyond we would do well to call integration. It is not a deduction. The integrative feat links otherwise unrelated particulars together in a pattern whose coherence far exceeds a logical consistency that we could express entirely in words. The integration transforms the clues, even as it transforms our selves and our world. Where there was an inscrutable surface in a Magic Eye puzzle, now dolphins swim in an underwater paradise.

On the old model of knowing, the only thoroughly approved method of extending knowledge is deduction. In deductive reasoning you move from statements that are called premises to a statement called a conclusion. The conclusion of a deductive argument follows necessarily from the premises: if the premises are true, the conclusion has to be true also. This is what we call an inferential connection. We have come to associate the clearest of these with the height of rationality. Does this mean that integration, because it is not deductive, is irrational?

No. An inferential structure is not impoverished by the addition of unspecifiable features of our knowing. Rather, the inferential structure, if thought to express the act exhaustively, is the thing that impoverishes our knowing. Integration is not irrationality; it is transformed rationality. The dog wags the tail; the tail doesn't wag the dog.

What actually happens in the act of knowing is that the relationship between clues and pattern, subsidiaries and focus, is not one of premises and deduced conclusion. When you see Magic Eye dolphins, you cannot fully express in words all the particulars on which you rely, nor all that the focus includes, let alone a step-by-step procedure you followed to move from the one to the other. You cannot express the particulars as premises, because prior to the actual act of integration—before your first-ever seeing of Magic Eye dolphins—you are in no position to articulate the very things that you must rely on if you are to integrate to the pattern. If anything makes the particulars premise-like, it might be that the focus is conclusion-like. Using the terminology, then: before you can put the "conclusion" in words, you must already be relying on the "premises" that are only premises or clues in light of the "conclusion" you have yet to uncover and express! Logical inference is too impoverished a procedure to capture the grand thing that is going on in the act of knowing.

An integration reconciles clues that on the surface may have appeared contradictory. It's as if when you focus on the particulars, you are interpreting them in light of one vision of the rational, and when you toggle to rely on the particulars as clues, you make the switch to interpreting them in light of a vision of the rational that is embedded in the focus. Moving from one to the other involves changing camp.

After the first discovery, yes, we are able to specify some of the clues we rely on. If pianists couldn't describe in words some of the things they do in order to play piano well, there could be no piano teaching and no new pianists. But those descriptions could hardly be premises from which the result could be necessarily derived. They function more as maxims guiding the learner's efforts, clues that the student embodies in the struggle to grasp a new coherence.

But even if all the clues could be articulated and the procedure exhaustively specified, in the actual act of integration the knower does not (cannot) articulate them but rather relies on them or embodies them to achieve the focus.

But the act is not illogical or irrational or mystical, even though it is awesome. We know well what it feels like to integrate. We have only to recall numerous experiences of skilled integration we execute in every dimension of our lives. It is quite ordinary, because it is fundamentally human. It is skill, knowing how, lived-in knowledge, not irrational mysticism. Riding a bike is not a mystical or irrational experience. And though you can specify a mathematical formula that represents what the biker does to keep his balance, it would be ludicrous to view the formula as requisite to the achievement, or to view the achievement as irrational apart from its specification. What counts is that the biker lives the formula, whether or not he or she can verbalize it.

The act of integration, I think it is better to say, is not irrational but transrational. In it our sense of what is rational is transformed, not violated. For what happens is that, on the way to a fresh discovery, the knower must already, subsidiarily, come to embody the clues as they are interpreted according to the rationality of the end result. Without this occurrence, the end result is unattainable. And this means that, when the knower arrives at the integrative coherence, she finds herself already embracing a rationality which is shaped by the reality that she has come to know. Everything, we can feel, we now see in a fresh light. And if we had held to our old standards of rationality, we would never have seen it.

Is logic, then, useless? Please—I teach logic! Because we are humans who put words on things in a systematic way and articulate and draw out consequences, representing our efforts verbally dramatically extends our hold on the real and evokes fresh prospects. Far from inhibiting our laying hold of the real, verbalization extends our intuitive capacities to do so. If we go through life inarticulate and inference-impoverished, we will not accomplish much. Logic, like any tool, when used properly extends our influence.

Lest this sound more radical and frightening than it is, let's talk about an everyday sort of experience. Remember my father's zucchini that fell off the windowsill in the night and turned on the water faucet? Prior to venturing forth to the kitchen, I had at my disposal no premises from which I might reason to that conclusion. The whole thing eluded me. The concept of zucchinis having within their capacity to turn on water faucets would have seemed to me to fall outside what might be rationally expected of a zucchini. My horizon of rationality—my grasp of the real—was that night irrevocably and hilariously expanded. It's as ordinary and as common an occurrence as that.

Seeing integration as richer than inference, and seeing rationality as embedded subsidiarily in the next integrative coherence, ought to lead us to rethink learning and discovery. It has implications for the way we teach. I believe that, in communicating to you, my words and my inferential structure are critical tools. It's just that there's more to it. This is why I said to you at the beginning that getting every word should not necessarily be your agenda as you read this book—that learning can occur even if you don't fully grasp each word. You can get the feel of the thing. For a teacher, this is both humbling and liberating. My words don't guarantee the success of your learning, but neither do they prevent it. My words work less like premises and more like evocative clues, even when I structure them as premises.

■ Knowing Auto Mechanics and God: Integration Richer than Inference

If you and I waited for a fully reasoned proof of our mechanic's reliability, we would never get our car fixed. It makes more sense to see that in taking my car to him I am trusting to a reality with a certain internally coherent character. I am letting the conclusion shape my premises. To take my car to him is a kind of commitment to the coherence of a vision of his integrity as real, good, and reliable. It may involve me in "getting off the dime"—calling a halt to questioning or to my quest for certainty. It is a lived epistemic extending of ourselves to embrace a fresh sense of the real and rational.

Knowing God is like this. I heard my friend James tell about his experience of coming to know God. When he was a boy of eleven years, his father was shot in a fight at the bar on Christmas Eve. In that moment he became the ranking man of the family, and an angry one too. Later, when he was grown, his mother contracted terminal cancer. He attempted at various points to end his own life. One time he purposely drove his truck into a brick wall. James lived an angry question thrown at God. How could a good God let this happen?

Listening to James tell this story, I wondered how he ever could have come to trust Christ. But he went on to say this: "I heard the good news about Jesus Christ—that he died for my sin, and that I could trust him to save me, even after death. It wasn't that my questions received a direct answer; it's that the questions I had had didn't seem to matter anymore. I gave my life to Christ."

When James came to feel that his questions didn't matter anymore, a transformation in his sense of the rational was underway. If God is who he says he is, and ruler enough and powerful enough and loving enough to come after me and buy me back, then he is not the sort of being of whom I demand answers. He is the one entitled to answers from me.

I can't think of much worse than having your father shot on Christmas Eve. Christians who move forward in knowing God can reasonably feel that they don't have much to say in the face of extreme injustice and pain. Sometimes the pain engulfs us and deadens our sense of God's presence.

But Christians trust and long for a God who reveals himself as the lawgiver and judge of the universe, who is already at work, and who promises at some point in the future to make himself fully known to all the world, and in that moment, to right all wrongs. Jesus teaches his followers to pray, "Your kingdom come. . . ."

Pain, I am learning firsthand, is not the ultimate evil I sometimes think it is. Nor is it a given that pain testifies against God's reality, love, or power. C. S. Lewis said, "God whispers in our pleasures . . . but shouts in our pains: it is His megaphone to rouse a deaf world." That has often been my experience. On the surface, to one who resists knowing God, this appears incomprehensible. But integrating to the God represented in the Bible, to Jesus, who "for the joy set before him endured the cross, scorning its shame, and sat down at the right hand of the throne of God"—such a pattern offers a profounder rationality. And in part it involves me in holding out for something that is not yet.

September 11, 2001, is a date none of us will forget. In fact, we refer to the hideous attacks of terrorists that destroyed two towers of the World Trade Center simply as "September 11." We felt as if we had looked evil in the face. A student of mine, a single mother, asked me that day, "How can I help my teenaged daughter, who says she doesn't believe in God, to process this?" The response I gave occurred to me even as I said it: This horror is not one that denies God's existence or the reality of good. That will happen only if we ever come to view such an event as good or of indifferent moral value, if we were to view it and feel no moral outrage. Human outrage at evil confirms God's reality, for there is no other way to account for the passion we feel. This is profoundly rational.

In the months following September 11, we witnessed another profound rationality. Out of the despicable crater at Ground Zero continued to grow all manner of good. We the people fell in love with the young husband who, with a favorite phrase, "Let's roll!" led fellow flight passengers to thwart terrorist attempts to crash the plane into the White House, whose wife stood bravely representing his heroic sacrifice by her presence at the president's address to Congress. My daughters' high school collected money; our church youth group did the same by means of a car wash. We hugged our children and spouses more closely. With remorse for past indifference, we honored the faithful service of firefighters. We listened to and wept with story after story. I remember one widow telling, some months later, how her entire block of neighbors had rallied around her family to care for her and her children's needs, not just for a week, but for as long as their services were needed. It was she who I remember saying, "Out of this horrible tragedy has grown tremendous good."

On one scheme of rationality, this makes no sense. All of us, I think, were both surprised by it, and also confirmed in our sense of what it means to be human. It takes submission to a grander scheme, on which it makes profound sense. There are always limits to the applicability of the law of noncontradiction, we might say. Its applicability depends at any moment on the aptness of our definition of the terms, and that grows out of the aptness of our sense of rationality at the time. We must humbly admit always that our grasp of the rationality of the real may need to be expanded or transformed.

Every human act of integration moves us from one rationality to a profounder one. The process is only partially expressed in an inference from premises to conclusion. To advance our grasp of the real is to allow our sense of the rational to conform to a reality that we have yet to grasp. If we are not open to this, we are blind to further knowledge. Critical acts of knowing, whether of auto mechanics or God, share this feature in common.

For Further Thought and Discussion

Think of examples. You have by now thought up several of your own experiences of coming to know. Think about them again.

- Were they more aptly described as integrations rather than deductions?
- How was your sense of what's rational or reasonable to expect of the real reshaped in the process?
- In what sense could you say that you could specify the conclusion and only later specify the premises?
- Do you find this upsetting or liberating?

Consider rationality. What do you think it means to be rational?

Apply these thoughts to your thinking about knowing God.

- How does what has been described here ring true to your experience in knowing God? In what ways does it not fit your experience?

PART III

. . . To Rely
on Clues . . .

Knowing
is the responsible human struggle
to rely on clues
to focus on a coherent pattern
and submit to its reality.

11

The Clues in Our World

The Dots We Connect
into a Meaningful Pattern

If we have been in the habit of thinking of knowledge merely as true and justified statements, we have probably been blind to the many tacit features that are essential to the act of knowing. One of them is the human effort of integration. Another is the ongoing presence of subsidiary knowledge, on which we rely to achieve a further focus. We need a fresh model of knowing that accredits these tacit dimensions, and we need to be retrained to recognize them. It isn't that subsidiary knowledge wasn't there; in fact, we've been relying on it the whole time we've been blind to it.

In the Magic Eye experience we saw that before our integrative shift, what we were looking at was a computer-generated collection of colored shapes. After that shift, we were looking at dolphins. We were looking somehow through the particulars to focus on a pattern beyond. The once-disconnected particulars now are connected meaningfully within the focus, and subsidiary to it. We see them now as parts of a whole.

Before the shift ever occurred, we relied on the directions to guide us to see the particulars in such a way that we would eventually come to the focus. When we enacted, bodily, what its creator told us to do, we came to rely on the shapes on the page to integrate into a pattern, and then we saw the dolphins.

■ The Telltale Oddness of Clues

Thinking about knowledge that we rely on, subsidiary knowledge, is especially difficult. By definition, we do not focus on it in our integrative achievement. As a result of that integration, the subsidiaries come to be so close to us, even part of us, that they are hard to see and thus difficult to articulate.

Subsidiaries are like our peripheral vision; in fact, peripheral vision is normally subsidiary knowledge. By definition you can't focus on your peripheral vision! But you rely on it all the time. (That's why the state police test drivers for it!) So in a way it's odd to talk about subsidiaries. Or if you do, you have to realize that your talking about them is not the same as your experience of them.

On the way to achieving a pattern, before we ever reach it, and if we are ever to reach it, we begin to rely subsidiarily on the particulars that previously we were simply looking at. We must struggle past looking at them to get inside them in a way that defies verbal expression. It has to happen that we start relating to them in this alternative way for our act of knowing ever to be achieved.

Clues are such odd things! If ever we had a modernist dream of totally explicit knowledge, of the possibility of keeping ourselves within the walls of a fortress of knowledge that we grasp with utter clarity, clues should puncture that dream. For clues are prime examples of knowledge that cannot fully be put into words, and that certainly cannot be thoroughly justified. What makes a clue a clue? (Think of the last mystery you read.) You couldn't really say with complete clarity what a clue is until after the mystery is solved. And by the time you can articulate that clue, that is, once you have solved the mystery or fought through to the pattern, you no longer are relying on the clue as a pointer to what you do not know. In relying on a clue we assign to it a significance beyond what it appears on the surface to have, and beyond what we can fully understand or explain. We don't know yet exactly what that significance is. Yet our unspecifiable sense of that significance guides us to our discovery.

■ The Surface Features of Our World

In thinking about the Magic Eye, we identified three main clusters of clues on which we rely in our integration to a pattern. The most obvious set of items-turned-subsidiaries were the particulars on the surface of the page. They are things outside of us, in our world. Our acts of knowing connect the dots, so to speak, of our world. Before the connecting, the particulars in question bear no obvious relationship to each other. After the connecting, the significant pattern that emerges is rooted in the world.

One of the things that happens with the things in our world as we integrate them is that we assign them a significance as figure or as ground. In the Magic Eye, some of the surface particulars become part of the three-dimensional dolphins. The rest become part of the background in front of which the dolphins play.

It's as if you were faced with doing a dot-to-dot puzzle in which the surface of the page was littered with dots, only some of which were the ones to be singled out and connected. Before you could successfully complete the puzzle, you had to figure out which were the significant dots, the ones meant to be connected in order to reveal the hidden pattern. I don't actually know of any puzzles like this, but it might be like having to crack a code before you could connect the dots.

When does noise become music? How do you distinguish static from a signal as you tune your radio? In the movie *The Hunt for Red October*, sonar man Jonesy listens intently to the noise coming through his earphones. He speeds up what he hears; he slows down what he hears. A sailor in training standing nearby hears nothing. But Jonesy's skilled ears detect a pattern that offers the critical clue concerning the Soviet submarine's propulsion system. His ranking officer rightly praises his risky postulation. Jonesy's skill enables him to distinguish a telling figure from its background.

A member of the crew in another movie, *The Matrix*, looks up from his computer screen of cascading numbers and says to Neo, "I don't see numbers any more, just blondes, brunettes, and redheads." He had so completely mastered the skill of deciphering patterns that the intermediary, interpretive step was no longer necessary.

Think of doctors reading X-rays. They see things that they point out to us, and I at least have only their word to go by in assigning significance to the light and dark areas on the film. "Your daughter has a slipped femoral epiphysis," a pediatric orthopedic surgeon told me when Stephanie was ten; "—see?" I drew a similar blank years earlier when the doctor put the stethoscope in my ears and on my bulging middle and told me I was hearing my baby's heartbeat. Doctors are trained to pick out patterns from the surface features of the world.

So are you. Think of any number of patterns that you have detected. When is music rock and roll? Country? Hip-hop? Scat? Jazz? When is it Scarlatti? Vivaldi? Chopin? Debussy? How can you tell whether it's modern art or just an accident? When is a couple "in love" or "just friends"? When is your roommate's behavior sensible or senseless? Is he insane? Or is he a genius? Or what is the significance of what he is doing? Is he planning your surprise birthday party? Or is he performing a psych experiment? Each of these assessments involves my assigning "figure" significance to some features of my experience, and "background" significance to others.

Which rattles in my car are harmless, and which noises spell dire and costly consequences? I cannot tell. But Jeff can. I'm probably better than he would be, however, at weeding my garden. Which plants should be there, and which plants should be pulled out? I don't even trust my husband with that one!

In no way is our personal contribution some arbitrary conferral of significance, even though it is profoundly a personal assigning. It is we who must initiate and value. It involves our personal choice. It often calls for rigorous training to develop personal skill. But nobody involved in the examples I have given above would see this personal effort as arbitrary, even if it is risky. An expert is not an autocrat. Hard as it occasionally may be to make the distinction, we feel it right to draw one between being visionary and being delusional. I may not connect any old dots I please. I must develop the skill and sensitivity to connect the right ones.

Optical illusions, such as the one in which we see either the duck or the rabbit, or the one in which we see the young woman or the old one, succeed in puzzling us because we have been given less than the usual amount of clues. In more ordinary cases of perception, we have more to work with. It would be ludicrous to conclude, on the basis of the illusions, that we may draw the lines of reality according to our private preference.

In every act of knowing, then, we rely on the surface features of our world. We attend to them carefully, climbing into them in search of a meaningful pattern. Our effort is rewarded with a three-dimensional entity fraught with significance that separates itself from the pack and is there.

▌ Knowing Auto Mechanics and God: Relying on the World's Clues in Finding a Pattern

When it comes to knowing my auto mechanic, you already know the pieces of my world that I integrated to the focus, Jeff is a good mechanic to choose to care for my car. Here was a big one at the start: Jeff, the kid who fixed cars in his garage, didn't charge much. That's no longer true, now that he is the grown-up owner of his own gas station. But other features are still true and still deemed significant by me. A big one: he still picks up cars from the seminary where we work. Not only is this a tremendous convenience, but it also indicates something really good about his character and reliability. He's faithful over a long period of time, and he gets a lot of business from my colleagues, who are people I trust. His mother speaks well of him; his father works for him. Now I think that's significant.

What about my friend's complaint that everytime she takes her car to Jeff, he finds more to fix than she asked him to fix? Well, there's more than one possible interpretation of that. Perhaps he's trying to make extra money, or perhaps he's indifferent to her pocketbook, as my friend thinks. But perhaps what happened between them was prompted by his being conscientious. The latter interpretation fits well with my integrated pattern. I dismiss some of her comments as background, not part of the pattern.

I rarely see Jeff. But my husband brings my car home from the seminary, and the steering no longer whines, and oil no longer spreads on the garage floor. And my bank account takes what I deem a reasonable dive. It's almost as if I see Jeff at work.

What are some of the features of my world that point to the pattern of knowing God? I see order and harmony and beauty in the world. Beauty is really there, says author Annie Dillard. I see disorder and frustration, too. I see that the Bible's story of creation marred by human rebellion, groaning for God's redemption and restoration, makes sense of both.

I see that humans everywhere worship something, and that most humans hope that their efforts will vindicate them before some ultimate tribunal. I see also that people don't even live up to their own standards, let alone to the standards of whatever God they worship. I see that the Bible tells me that I can never be right with God on the basis of my own performance; I will always fall short. It tells me I must claim the free gift of God that is Jesus paying for my penalty with his death and resurrection two thousand years ago. It tells me that this Jesus is the only way to God, and that the only way to know Jesus is through God's telling us about him in the Bible, and God the Holy Spirit's making me understand. What the Bible tells me makes sense of my experience that Christianity alone is different from all other futile efforts to reach God.

I see a world so utterly reliable when people interact with it that we can even write mathematical laws. Johannes Kepler labored for years in search of formulaic perfection, because he thought the planets were that reliable. He was right. I can always count on spring coming, on the sun rising. We can predict eclipses with complete precision. I can count on an apple tree bearing apples and a blueberry bush producing blueberries, and not vice versa. I can count on

my grass dying in a drought, unless I water it. The Bible tells me it's not impersonal laws that run things, but a personal and perfect Being whose "Here's the
way it's going to be!" is so much the law that things always happen the way he
says, and whose word is so steadfastly faithful that Kepler could describe his
faithfulness in a formula without remainder! I've learned to see every feature
of creation, as John Calvin says, as God's clothes. They move because he acts.
There is nothing in between.

Could the world be not God's clothes, but God, as some pagan religions hold?
This makes less sense of my experience. If all that is real is God, then either God
is not good, or evil is good. What is, is good, and is God. But that makes no
sense. Recently a distraught mother drowned her five children, one by one. My
stomach churns at the thought. I can't call a murdered child good. I cannot call
it God. I can look at a murdered child and bemoan the human brokenness that
brought it about and long for the promised day when God makes all wrongs
right. It makes more sense to see ourselves and our world in broken relationship to God, rather than as God. Of course that means God must be a person,
rather than a force, and persons rightly expect things of you. Rather than face
this painful thought, many people opt for the force. But the question is not which
is more comfortable, but which makes better sense of my experience.

Is it difficult to understand how God would allow there to be a murdered
child? Of course. But if God did not exist, how could I explain my moral outrage at this evil? When we experience something that doesn't seem to fit, and
especially when that causes us agony, we find ourselves quite naturally rethink-
ing our integrations. We have eventually to make a decision about its "status"
with respect to our integration.

But we do this all the time. When scientists work with chemicals in the lab,
their results are never small integers, ratios of two or three to one. But they
decide that their 1.999s and 1.003s are justifiably reduced to 2 and 1 (*significant* digits—remember?). If a student came up instead with 1.85 and 1.23, the
teacher might justifiably tell the student to do the lab again.

Sometimes the pattern isn't quite clear. And sometimes we are mistaken.
Constellations are connected dots of a sort. And people who trust horoscopes
to predict the future believe in the significance of their connection.

Surprising particulars of our world can also prompt revised integrations or
new ones. Every day that I walk before God tells me something new about
him—something new about his world and about me and about his plan. My
knowing of him is continually being shaped.

Coming to know God involves "tip offs" that we get from our daily lives.
Recently I heard of a young man who came to trust Christ because of a broken

leg! A high school football player, he had worked hard to prepare for his big senior year. In the first game of the season, he was carried off the field on a stretcher and didn't play the rest of the season. "There must be more to life," he reasoned. His broken leg led him to question the way he had been assigning significance to the features of his life. It led him to search for something that he didn't yet know. What he found was Jesus.

I rely on the particulars of my world for my knowledge of Jeff. I rely on the particulars of my world to detect the pattern of the God of the Bible. Knowing God and other ordinary acts of knowing share this in common.

For Further Thought and Discussion

Consider clues. Think for yourself about clues. Do you agree that they have the puzzling feature of being used before we can articulate them? Why is it therefore important to include our reliance on clues in our model of knowing?

Consider rationality. What do you think it means to be rational?

Revisit the movie *The Hunt for Red October.* This is one of my favorite movies. Like many others, it chronicles an act of coming to know.

- When is Jack Ryan's "Oh! I see it!" moment?
- What are some of the clues that trigger his integrative pattern?
- How risky is his commitment to his pattern?
- In what ways does he, by means of his pattern, more fully engage reality?

89

12

The Clues in My Body

The Lived Body Sense that Anchors Our Knowing

The clues we integrate to a focus include features of our world. They also include features of our body.

When we struggle to see the dolphins in the Magic Eye, we must make our eyes focus beyond the surface of the page. Our eyes focus when the line of vision of the one eye converges with the line of vision coming from the other. Right now my eyes' vision lines are converging on the screen of my computer. If I shift my focus to my hands, the point of convergence moves closer to me. If I look up at the bookshelf six feet beyond my computer, the point of convergence of the two lines of my eyes' vision moves farther away. If I look beside the bookcase into the full-length mirror on the door, my focal point moves even farther out, perhaps another six feet beyond the surface of the mirror.

Now, I'm forty-nine. That means I need reading glasses! No longer as supple as they once were, my eyes can't pull my focal point in close to me the way they used to. If I peer over my glasses at the computer screen, I can barely read the blurry words. Don't get old, if you can avoid it.

The fact that our eyes each have different lines of vision is what makes us see things in three dimensions. Old-fashioned stereopticons were invented, I am presuming, when some enterprising photographer strapped two cameras together side by side. When you look at the stereopticon card, you see two virtually identical photos, say, of Festival Hall at the 1904 World's Fair in St. Louis, side by side. Put the card in the stereopticon and hold it close to your eyes, and you see the hall in three-dimensional glory.

We know a lot about our eyes' focusing. But we usually only think about it when we enter middle age—or when we encounter Magic Eyes. When we first come across a Magic Eye, and read the directions, we're likely to react in surprise and consternation. How can we be expected to make our eyes focus beyond the surface of the page? Or perhaps the creator just told us to hold the picture against our face and then slowly move it away. We don't know enough about our focal points to know how to move them into this new situation at will.

We follow the directions and we succeed. We may yet have no clue what we did right. Yet if we hadn't done it right, we never would have seen three-dimensional dolphins. After practice, we learn to recognize and control our eyes' movement.

Our bodies are the most amazing things. But here I am not talking about the fabulous job kidneys do, or brains. It is also amazing to think of how they bear on our knowing. Our bodies are, for us as knowers, a vast set of experiences that we know almost exclusively as they bear on other things. We know our fingers as so many capacities to type, cook, strum a guitar, fashion a clay pot. We have lived knowledge of them. My daughter's viola teacher says to her, It's not your mind that needs to learn the intervals on the strings; it's your fingers. And they do. If you can touch-type on a keyboard, your fingers know where to go when you type the word *fingers*. Were I to ask you which fingers you used, and in what order, I'm willing to bet that you couldn't answer without wiggling your digits in the air at an imaginary keyboard.

As we gain a skill, our body knowledge is shaped and developed. Then, we add tools. In our skilled use of them, it's as if our body extends to their edges. We interiorize them, or we indwell them. We live in them as we do in our fingers. We rely on what the car feels like as we skillfully weave down a busy interstate.

It is the exception, rather than the rule, when we think of our bodies as objects. How many times have you heard people say something like this: "You never think about your back until something goes wrong with it!"? It's when something goes wrong that we stop relying on, living in, our body, and focus on it instead. The same is true of any tools we have embodied. Heidegger originated the example of the door to the classroom: You are late for class. You run to the door, open it, and rush in. Were you thinking about the doorknob? When might you notice the doorknob? When it turns out to be locked, or it comes off the door in your hands! These examples help us see the difference between focal and subsidiary awareness with respect to body clues. And it helps us identify from our own experience what it is to have a lived awareness of things.

Take any truth claim you can think of. In some way it is embedded in your body. Have you heard someone say, "I can't read without a highlighter"? Or "I can't learn without pictures"? Or "I won't remember if I don't write it down"? There are bodily features of our most abstract knowings. They are supported not only by obvious body efforts. They crest the multitudinous layers of indwelt and body-extending tools and constructs that I have appropriated subsidiarily in pursuit of ever farther focal patterns.

As a teacher, I take seriously this lived aspect of knowing and learning. I've decided that my students learn best and try hardest when they know I love them, when they don't feel threatened. I give out lots of encouragement. I receive lots of hugs. And I am teaching the most abstract of verbal skills. I also believe strongly that the most important aspect of my teaching is my excitement. My students continue to brave the rigors of deep and complex questions with courage and delight because they knew my encouragement and my excitement. I taught their bodies as well as their minds. A student recently paid me a backwards compliment: he said, "You're not safe!" He meant that I blend my scholarly and what you might call my motherly approach in such a way that he can't tell where the boundaries are. Yet that is what binds his heart to learning. As important as *logos* is *ethos*, Aristotle would say.

We know very well the connectedness of our ideas and our bodies. Happy thoughts bring inner peace and joy. Anxious thoughts can, over a period of time, damage our body health. Our thoughts leave their footprints in the wrinkles that crease our faces, for good or ill. And our general approach to life graphically impacts the claims we are able to affirm, the skills we develop, and the action we take. We all recognize that there can be more- or less-healthy approaches to life. Our approach to life is our body-based, lived feel of things.

When I feel I can trust somebody, something inside me relaxes. When something goes wrong, something inside feels not right. We talk about feeling comfortable with someone or with a state of affairs. This is a reference to our body sense.

We trust our body sense to guide our judgment. In the movie *Star Wars*, Han Solo has a way of saying, "I've got a bad feeling about this!"—as the trash compactor creaks ominously, or the sides of the cave turn out to be soft. We laugh because he might have had the feeling sooner and spared himself some trouble. We laugh because he expresses what we've been feeling for a long time. But all of us navigate partly in terms of this lived sense. We would do well to pursue seriously and intentionally its cultivation.

■ Knowing Auto Mechanics and God: A Lived Sense of the Real

Ask me about Jeff as an auto mechanic, and my body-sense is a feel-pretty-good one. When my car breaks down, my body longs to get the car to him. I don't start to feel right until I know it's in his care. Then I relax.

Suppose Jeff began repeatedly to forget to pick up my car at the seminary, or the things I asked him to fix didn't get fixed. The faulty symptoms didn't change noticeably when he was supposed to have fixed something. Suppose I heard of his being mixed up in some shady dealings. Suppose his gas station started to look slovenly. I would be relying on my senses for all these experiences. I would also be growing an uncomfortable feeling in the pit of my stomach. If you asked me about Jeff as an auto mechanic, I would get this feeling.

Is it too much of a stretch to say that we rely on bodily clues when we know God? I think not. Some people have thought that there is no such thing as religious experience. Some have thought religious experience was only mystical or irrational. I think bodily clues are included in our experience of God, and I don't think of it as a mystical experience. For example, all of us have known moments of glory, brushes with transcendence, whether in sports or in music, mountains or sunsets, creative acts, childbirths, or acts of heroism. Those experiences have a bodily dimension to them. We are caught up, transported. Something in us cries out for transcendence, as our fingers might itch to touch velvet, or our feet to dance to Scott Joplin. To what do these body longings point?

Bringing bodies in line with God's words involves obedience. Obedience is lived truth. And I can sense within my body the effect of that alignment. I read in the Bible: "Don't be deceived, God cannot be mocked: whatever a person sows, that will he reap." My body tells me that this is generally true! If I do things that the Bible says are right and good, my body senses the shalom promised. If I choose to disobey what God says, I may know body pleasure for a time. But it comes to a painful end. I could give you far too many examples of this. I'll let you cite your own.

Shalom is the well-being that comes only as God gives it, and only as his graciously given commands come to living expression in our lives. His "Here's the way it is," the Bible, is like a how-to-operate manual for humans and the world. When we orient our lives toward him and align them with his words, we can taste shalom. The analogy I have in my head is of one of those jointed paper skeleton decorations that offer dubious delight to our Halloweens: if you were to grab the collapsed skeleton by the head, lift it up and give it a shake, all the sections of the skeleton would slide into their proper place. Following through on the First Commandment—No other gods before me—is like grabbing our lives by the topmost point. The rest of our lives slide to their proper place. And the lived body experience that results, the alignment we can call shalom, feels good.

I hardly need to say that life isn't that simple. For starters, the Bible also tells the story of human rebellion, human brokenness and need. The human is still functioning, but the human is warped. Even apart from the bentness, we would have needed God to know God. As it is, knowing God can feel more like a fight than an easy, natural recognition. It can feel as if we have to go against ourselves to be true to ourselves.

The Bible also helps me to understand how bent humans can function in light of God's gift of Jesus Christ to pay the debt I owe to God. Actually, my undeniable disobedience led me to a richer experience of God's grace. I was forced to be honest about my disobedience. I could no longer delude myself into thinking I was a good little girl for whom God's intervention was only a token effort. Once I had my nose rubbed in the awfulness of my behavior, I felt very much that I could not redeem myself. It would have to be God. Then I came to appreciate in a fresh and profound way the greatness of Christ's payment and the unconditionality of God's grace. I felt deeply loved and accepted, and that there would be nothing I could do that would change his being for me. It was tremendously humbling, freeing, and joy-giving. And I felt it in my body.

Human action is lived truth (or falsehood). Body experience is not just what it feels like from the inside. It is also what I do—how the truth comes to expression in my life. I believe this chair is solidly built. I live that belief, I embody that belief, in my sitting on it. If it were not for this connection, movies could never be made. Movies rely on communicating beliefs through action. My true commitments come to expression in my action. That's why we all can sense the presence or absence of hypocrisy.

Knowing, we might say, is incarnated. Plato just turned over in his grave. But it's the kind of view of knowing that I think a bodily resurrected Jesus would confirm. Not to mention a world-making, embodied human–making God.

I embody my knowledge of Jeff by sending my car to him. It's that simple. I embody my knowledge of God by trying to do what he says. That's why the Bible makes short work of those who claim to know God and don't do what he says. Knowledge is lived, bodily. Obeying God's commands is bodily living the truth. I can give you one guaranteed way to know God: obey him. As you live the truth, you are most likely to come to know the focus of your epistemic act.

Notice the interesting thing about obedience. We don't focus on the obedience; we move through it to focus on God. Believers find, or ought to be able to find, that you can get too fixated on doing what you are supposed to do, so much so that you can lose sight of a gracious, relational God. It would be like fixating so religiously on my husband's words that a wooden rigidity actually comes between me and him. ("But you SAID . . . !"—words sadly familiar.) On the other hand, taking words seriously is a profound way of coming to know someone, whether God or spouses (or auto mechanics). Locating obedience, lived truth, in the subsidiary, as opposed to the focal, makes sense of this dynamic.

Even as all other skills live in their bodily roots, so the skill of knowing, even as it pushes out the frontiers of our body, never severs its fundamental connection. It is an embodied me who knows Jeff, and who enacts my knowledge of him by sending my car to him and expecting it to be fixed. It is an embodied me that proves out the truth of the God of the Bible in my obedient or disobedient behavior.

For Further Thought and Discussion

Identify your lived body experiences. Think once more over the collection of acts of coming to know and skills that you have thought about over the last chapters.

- For at least one of these, describe some of the particular body experiences on which you rely.
- Can you remember how your own body experiences were taught and extended as your grew in your knowledge?

Consider our Western philosophical legacy. Why did I say that this chapter would make Plato turn over in his grave?

Consider the Bible's worldview. Many people have mistakenly believed that Christianity was a disembodied religion. This has resulted most likely from our reading our Western philosophical legacy into Scripture. How do the Bible's themes of creation, incarnation, resurrection, and restoration, all of which have to do with God's interaction with a tangible world and embodied persons, affirm the role our bodies play in knowing, and vice versa?

Assess your own perceptions of Christian religious experience. Is the view of the role of the body in knowing, even in knowing God, presented in this chapter, new to you? Do you think these claims make sense, or do you reject them? Why? Can you supply other examples of bodily clues involved in knowing?

13

The Clues in the Directions

The Role of Authoritative Guides in Knowing

When we talked about the Magic Eye, we said that there was a third set of clues, in addition to the clues of the world and the clues of our body. The third set is the directions. At the point when we first encounter the Magic Eye, the directions are perhaps our most important clue. It's all we have to go on at the outset. Without them, we can't even understand that the picture is a puzzle. We simply wouldn't know what to do with the picture. Its gaudy, official presence in a newspaper or book may tip us off that the game is afoot. But we simply would have no way, apart from the directions, of figuring out what the game is and in which direction to seek it.

The directions not only set the game, they also tell us what to do to play it. And what's more, we rely on them to tell us what it looks and feels like for us to play it. We rely on guides to interpret and correct our own body's experiences.

Before I gave birth to our first child, I was a complete skeptic about the physical possibility of breast-feeding. I couldn't imagine how anything like milk would come out of me, or how I could ever be in a position to get it to happen. I will never forget when the nurse brought me freshly cleaned and swaddled Starr in the wee hours of the night just after she was born. She told me what to do: "Put the baby to your breast and tickle her cheek. Human babies have one instinct—sucking." I did what she said, despite my staunch disbelief. I could see the baby sucking. But then I heard the nurse's words, which I will never forget: "There! She's getting it." Whatever my body was supposed to be doing, which I didn't at that time know how to recognize, let alone perform, it was doing. The nurse had said so. It was a pronouncement of blessing. My skepticism fled, and my sense of wonder took over. In a few months I learned to recognize the body feelings that were the magic milk letdown—"No letdown, no milk," another nurse had said. I was guided to truth, and even to my own body experiences, by an authoritative word.

The Canadian Brass, an immensely talented and funny quintet, has spoofed the ballet: in their tuxes and sneakers, they tell the audience that they have never seen a ballet but would like to play a tribute to it. They have phoned their ballerina friend and asked her to describe ballet over the phone. (Here the guide is defective: she's kept from doing what would have to be done for there to be true learning.) They proceed to play exquisitely a medley of ballet music while simultaneously acting out the most outrageous moves! The riotous piece culminates with the tuba player playing his way through a slow somersault, ending flat on his back with the instrument's bell facing the audience! The Brass needed the ballerina to show them the moves, and then watch to tell them whether they are in fact doing it. But then, of course, the joke would have been spoiled.

Think of any skill that you can remember learning. Do you remember the words of a guide, someone who told you of the goal, and told you how to get there, and even told you what it feels like, or what you ought to be seeing?

■ We Need to Be Taught to See What Is There

My husband's and my former colleague and good friend Phil Long is not only adept at Old Testament studies, but is also a wonderful portrait painter. One time when his and our children were younger, I asked Phil if he would be willing to give all our kids an art lesson. He agreed. Down in our basement, he had us assemble drawing paper and pencils, and also a photograph of someone's face.

"Now," Phil began, "here's the big thing you need to know: you need to paint what you see!" He sat back, arms folded, grinning smugly as if he had uttered a profound and hitherto secret revelation. Our faces must have registered one big blank. But then came the interesting part: Phil started to teach us what we saw. "Look at the eyes. Do you see that there is a little dot of light? Look where it is with respect to the iris and the pupil. How could you draw that? And look at the whole eye: where are the big important lines? And what lines don't stand out so dramatically?" And so it continued.

One hour later, we had completed copying our photos. I simply couldn't believe what I saw on my own paper: my sketch, for the first time in my life, actually resembled the original! You could actually recognize the person I had sketched! I had needed to be taught how to see.

We labor under the misimpression that we see what we see, that seeing is believing, that either I see it or I don't. Not true. Not only artist hopefuls need to have their seeing trained. So do X-ray technicians, and pediatricians who diagnose ear infections. Once you start thinking about it, so do we all, in our many varied skillful pursuits.

Take the kitchen, for example. I had to have somebody teach me how to make bread. A dear father-friend gave me his bread recipe. He told me I had to knead it "until the dough feels like a baby's bottom." The words still guide my efforts. I needed my mother-in-law to teach me how to use a dough hook. "When the dough climbs the dough hook—like this—it's time to turn out the dough."

Cognitive therapists promote healing by getting their patients to think differently. Sometimes, apart from someone else's insistence and guidance, we don't even get it right about the thoughts in our own head. We need to be taught how to see.

Author Annie Dillard, in her Pulitzer Prize–winning novel, *Pilgrim at Tinker Creek*, in her marvelous chapter on seeing, says, "The lover can see, and the knowledgeable." Seeing is about what is there; we need to be guided to see what is there. We're not talking about inventing private constructions.

"The lover can see, and the knowledgeable." Loving is longing. Being knowledgeable involves training in skill. These are epistemic, integral aspects of knowing. And they require external, skilled, authoritative guidance. Knowing of any sort, I believe, involves such guidance. Are we being irresponsible as knowers to entrust our epistemic efforts to another's guidance? To submit to their authority? No. What would be irresponsible would be to deny our need of such guidance.

■ Why We Need Authoritative Guides

Why are guides so critical to knowing? I can think of at least three reasons. The first is that human knowing is rooted not, as the traditional model suggested, in certainties, but rather in subsidiaries—clues lived rather than verbalized lucidly. For us to live in them and through them, we can't look at them, and in some ways we are blind to them. Other people, especially those whose authority we sense is justifiable, can serve as mirrors in which we can and must see the clues closest to ourselves. Subsidiaries can be like backs, which, I think, cry out for the response of others, if they are to be massaged or anointed with sunscreen. Backs should make communal creatures of all of us. So should subsidiaries—so should knowing. We can move forward in some measure without such aid. But our full development as skilled, well-rounded knowers requires insight beyond our own.

Second, no clues on which we rely—world, body, or directions—are immune from error, and thus above needing interpreting by a qualified guide. The subsidiaries are indeed the roots of our knowing, but let us not glibly conclude that they are therefore mistake-free. Just because we have a felt sense does not mean that our felt sense is always right. We're not automatically right about either our body sense or about what we see or about what we think. More basic even than this, sometimes we need guides even to help us develop a body sense in the first place. This was true of my letdown reflex. The roots of our knowings must be trained and nurtured, as must our focal efforts. Coaches and guides have to interpret and teach us how to interpret even our own bodies. Without their authoritative input, we get our own selves wrong.

Third, knowing involves assigning significance to the features of our experience. Pattern making is inherently an exercise in value assignment. And successful access to the world depends on proper assignments. And proper assignments depend on expertise. And expertise requires a guide to teach us to see.

For me to pick out a pattern, I have to assign value to certain features of my experience and no value to others. At the point that this must start to happen in my act of knowing I am lacking the very sense of significance I need. I need an authoritative guide to point out to me what I cannot at that point see for myself. Phil Long taught me to assign value to the white light reflected off of eyeballs. It was then that I saw the pattern I needed to see.

The problem stage of a discovery comes when the knower assigns significance to a certain cluster of features of his experience, a significance that at that moment he can not fully articulate. Something strikes us as puzzling. Even more basic than being puzzled is simple noticing. Noticing is something we have to do in order to see what it is we are seeing. Our simplest perceptions involve us in assigning significance in order to see. Your parents or primary caregivers began this process for you. They said, "Ball!" and normed your world and shaped your seeing.

Once we have personally developed a skill, the authoritative word no longer seems to operate in a grand void, as it did when we were novices. Think again of your experience with the Magic Eye. After the first time, you hardly need to read the directions again, unless you're fishing for words to explain to somebody else what to do. We no longer have a sense of blindly trusting words we hardly understand. We have achieved our own pattern of world experiences and thus accessed the real. We now interpret aright for ourselves our body sense. But actually, in our personal success we have not left the guiding words behind. We have only come to live in the words, embody them. They are no longer outside us; they are inside us.

Even after the first occurrence, I still always assess significance in order to know, and that presupposes my ongoing active reliance on criteria for judgment. My ongoing acts of knowing continue to possess a normative aspect that guides and defines each occurrence. Every time that I return to sketching an eye, I will be looking for that white light and placing it with respect to the other colors of the eye I am trying to represent. Phil is now teaching in Canada, but I have internalized, embodied, his guidance.

Even when we are old hands, some word, some norm, guides our thought. I remember my father's maxim every time I set up a photograph with my camera. "Make sure there's some foreground, and don't put the subject in the middle of the picture." Whose words do you hear in your head at the junctures of your life?

When we think more broadly across the vast reaches of our truth claims, we can identify numerous guides, varying from subject to subject. For many things we believe, we can't remember the guides or the guiding moment. (When did your mom or dad teach you to identify a ball, and to distinguish it from the china figurine on the coffee table?) When you gain expertise in a certain area, your voice becomes the guiding word, your lived perceptions the expert feel of it. But your epistemic efforts continue to be guided, normed efforts. You have internalized the rightness that unlocks the world to you.

And embedded in every truth claim, even in every word, remains a normative aspect. We can apply it more or less correctly. The child uses the word *ball* and hurls the china figurine. Well, she got part of it right, the "hurl" part of it.

This little example, by the way, shows us the sobering fact that our words affect the world. Suppose in our value assigning we pick out a defective pattern. In doing this we can hurt the world. Wouldn't it be grand to import Chinese bush honeysuckle to the United States? I would like personally to choke the person who first had that idea. St. Louis woods are being overrun by bush honeysuckle, and wildflowers and tree saplings have been forced out of existence. We exercise sobering responsibility and hopefully good stewardship in our lifelong choosing of directions.

■ Responsible Stewardship rather than Epistemic Ultimacy

This means, in turn, that we would do well to choose wise guides. And indeed we all know this. We all know that with respect to any quest, some guides are more reputable than others. Whom do you trust when you choose a diamond, or a Persian rug? Whom do you trust to tell you what's wrong with your car's motor, or with your liver? If you wanted somebody to teach you to swing a golf club, and money was not a factor, whom would you choose? Your next-door neighbor? Or Tiger Woods?

Knowing involves trusting ourselves to authorities. This does not mean that our personal act of trust, no matter how perfect the authority we trust, is guaranteed to be mistake-free. Most authorities are not mistake-free, and most authorities have limited areas of expertise. But it is also the case that we are personally involved in assessing the weight and extent and accuracy of those whom we trust. We may be mistaken in our understanding of its claim; we may misapply it. So even if the authority is utterly trustworthy, our accurate understanding and apt appropriation of it depends on our skill and sensitivity. It is not as if we can set ourselves up as an ultimate authority. We get a lot of things right only as we let others stand in judgment upon our own perceptions. We are always personally engaged, but never personally ultimate. Or if we are, we incur stupidity.

This is a tricky process to describe, and one that I think we carry out better than any prescription for it that we could verbalize. (Skill, remember?) The picture that comes to my mind is of bats, who orient themselves and navigate forward by bouncing sound off any objects nearby. We trust the guidance of others to tell us where we are and how to move forward.

We have plenty of experience doing this. We speak of someone as gullible or skeptical, for example. In speaking this way, we are locating that person on a spectrum of proper or improper trust in a guide. We talk of "taking someone's words with a grain of salt." We talk of someone's book being the Bible for that field of skill or information. We are navigating by guides all the time, and exercising responsible agency simultaneously. In such a rich and complex mix of personal agency and rootedness in the real, neither the knower nor the authority need be seen as what we might call epistemically ultimate. It's not so much who trumps whom. It has more the feel of responsible stewardship.

■ Authority versus Authoritarianism

People in the Western tradition tend to have lots of issues when it comes to trusting authorities. It doesn't help that as children we may have had very painful experiences at the hands of our guides. But we have also become skittish at the hands of philosophy. The story of Western philosophy is our story. It includes a time in our coming of age when authority was painted as an illegitimate source of knowledge. It was noble, by contrast, to think for ourselves. And now in this postmodern milieu, we feel painfully that any decision to trust is discredited because deconstructable—reducible without remainder to factors of power.

The move to reject authority was warranted but not justified. Bad use of authority, we should see, does not entail the rejection of authority, for the rejection of authority is impossible. Bad use of authority entails the rejection of bad authority. The fact that some authorities are bad means that we need to exercise wisdom in our stewardship.

Our legacy has led us to read authority as authoritarianism, and seriously to be misled in requiring unconditioned freedom in every legitimate human act. We bristle at the word *authority*. That's why often in this chapter I have opted for the words *directions, guides, coaches*. But we must see that our actual dependence on authority remains.

If what I have been arguing about knowing is correct, knowing cannot happen without value assignment, and skill at such assignment requires insight other than our own. This was as true of the Enlightenment philosophers as it is of us. We never can remove ourselves totally from a matrix of authority, of words that norm our experience. Not to decide, not to trust an authority, is to decide, to submit to another authority.

Authoritarianism would be compelled or thoughtless submission in the absence of any felt sense of trustworthiness. But if you didn't trust Tiger Woods to teach you golf, who comes off looking like a fool? Trusting trustworthy authorities is good and responsible behavior in knowing. It is also unavoidable.

■ Knowing Auto Mechanics and God: Trusting the Authoritative Word

When it comes to the workings of an automobile, I have few independent thoughts, and even those are shaped by what somebody once said to me. I recognize a tire blowout, because I had one once. But even that experience was shaped by someone's words. I had heard people talking about blowouts.

When I actually had one, those words suited themselves to and shaped my experience with compelling force! I knew I had had a blowout the moment it happened.

My husband loves to listen to *Car Talk*, the public radio call-in show with Tom and Ray Magliozzi, two hilarious and very astute auto mechanics. They have an uncanny ability to diagnose both car problems and people problems. People describe their car's noises and behaviors; Tom and Ray are rarely stumped. They may be the last word in auto mechanics.

But for our old Taurus, Jeff's words are pretty much the norm. We have often asked him, "When does it make sense to get rid of this car?" He has replied, "If what you want is an old car for around town and for teaching kids to drive, hang on to this one a while longer." We do what he says.

He has helped me know how to identify the clunk in the right rear of the car. He told me it was the struts, which are shot. Now I hear the noise and think—struts. When having to choose between alternative routes, I opt for the smoother one. I also wonder if I should part with the money it would take to cure the problem, or save it for something I need more. My feeling tends to vary with the number of bumps in the road. Jeff's words have shaped my own body clues, and they shape my sense of the world and of the future.

When it came to knowing and trusting Jeff in the first place, we relied on the guiding words of several in the seminary community when we first came here. In acting on what they said and taking our cars to Jeff, we interiorized those directions. And we still live in light of them. It's not as if we've turned off our antennae about Jeff. If Jeff were convicted for odometer tampering, for example, or if money were stolen from our car while it was in the shop, we would of course be open to revising our commitment to these guiding words. But we don't approach Jeff with suspicion. Nor are we failing to exercise rational integrity if we don't. It is part and parcel of any epistemic act that the words of some guide directed our initial efforts, gave us eyes to see, and now have been interiorized by us.

When it comes to knowing God, I trust what the Bible says. In fact, I trust it to tell me what I'm feeling as well as what it leads to. You're wishing you had your neighbor's boat? That's coveting. Don't do it, or if you do it, expect to be miserable, and expect it to lead to further trouble. The Bible told me what to do when I first wanted to be right with God: "For God so loved the world that he gave his one and only Son, that whoever believes in him shall not perish but have eternal life." I took him at this word, and I still do, even in the temporary, relative absence of body-based or world-based confidence in its rightness. I expect to die, but I expect, because of his promise, that one day I will live again, and live forever. I have learned to trust the Bible to interpret to me my own experience. The result is that I understand myself more profoundly.

The God who claims the right to interpret my experience does not expect me to trust him blindly. The best authorities appeal to us across the whole spectrum of human experience and knowing. They are rational, testable, and practical. In the Bible, God calls his people to obey, but he also has given mighty acts as empirical testimony, such as making a path through the sea for the deliverance of the Jewish slaves from Egypt, and raising Jesus from the dead. And then he invites us to live in relationship with him and taste for ourselves the benefits of it. I trust him because I find him trustworthy.

When I first trusted Jesus as Savior, I was trusting the words of the Bible, as well as the words of my parents and teachers. Now that I have lived as a Christian for several decades, I have experiences of my own. But the very words of Scripture shape my experience. And I keep learning fresh ways in which to apply Scripture to my experience. It's as if I live the words of Scripture. And I am not alone. Even people who do not consider themselves Christians speak of "trying to live by the Golden Rule."

Scripture itself demonstrates that knowing rightly requires assigning the proper significance to events. The Bible chronicles a series of events. It also interprets those events. Jesus performs miracles; he then explains them. I love his question, asked with respect to John the Baptist: "What did you go out into the desert to see?" This is the kind of question an expert teacher asks. He then tells us, authoritatively, what it was we saw. Seeing is definitely not all there is to believing. Scripture models sound epistemology.

The Magic Eye creator's words of direction shaped my efforts, from a time even before I had any body experiences or world clues to speak of. The directions guided and normed my experience. When it comes to my car, Jeff's words carry the day. I make his words mine. They stand in judgment on both my experience and my world. When it comes to knowing God, God's words in Scripture guide and norm my experience. They tell me what I experience and what I ought to think of it. I seek to live in the words, and I know myself and my world better for this effort.

It is important to see that the fact that people rely on the Bible as an authoritative guide when it comes to knowing God in no way sets knowing God apart from any other ordinary act of knowing. Coming down to us from the Middle Ages has been the idea that the Bible contained revealed truth, and thus its claims were accessed by faith, while principles, say, of science were accessed by reason. When reliance on authority as a credible source of knowledge became disreputable, the religious enterprise was discredited also. By arguing that all human acts of knowing require authoritative guides, I hope you see that I mean to challenge this time-honored but false and unfortunate dichotomy. We trust our parents, we trust the nurse, we trust the Magic Eye directions, we trust the auto mechanic, we trust the piano teacher, we trust Scripture. If you like, you may call it faith. But you must call it faith when the topic is breast-feeding or golf or auto mechanics just as it is faith when the topic is God. We must also see that this is the stuff of reason. What is part and parcel of any human act of knowing we would do well to call rational, and just plain common sense. It's reasonable for me to trust Jeff. It is in the same way reasonable for me to trust Scripture.

For Further Thought and Discussion

Identify your guides. Think once more over the collection of acts of coming to know and skills that you have thought about over the last chapters.

- Can you remember how you came to place your trust in these guides?
- How did they guide you? How do they guide you now?
- Does your reliance on these guides negate your responsible involvement in the process? Why or why not?
- Can you also identify situations in which you were unwise in your choice of guides?
- What are some guidelines people follow in making wise choices of guides?

Consider your own response. How do you respond to the claims of this chapter concerning authority? Are these new thoughts to you? With what do you agree or disagree? Why?

Consider the implications for Christianity. The Christian religion has always been known to involve submission to an authoritative word in order to know God. How does the realization that such responsible submission is a feature of all knowing serve to link knowing God more closely with knowing anything? How does this affect your ideas about knowing God?

14

Integration Transforms the Clues

A Fresh Vision, a Fresh Feel, a Fresh Significance, a New Me

The integrative act of knowing shifts the way we relate to the particular features of our world, our selves, and our normative guides. When we integrate to a coherent focus, we change our manner of relating to the particulars. We shift from looking at them to looking through them. We perceive them no longer as unrelated particulars but as clues to the whole, profoundly related in the pattern. The way they feel from the inside seems to have no apparent relation to the way they were when they were outside us. Our integration transforms them.

Words provide such a glorious example of how the features of our acts of knowing shift as we move from looking at them to looking from them! The success of our effort shifts their status. No longer objects, they are tools. No longer walls, they are windows. No longer meaningless, they gain meaning.

My oldest daughter recently arrived home from a month in Guayaquil, Ecuador, where regular use of her Spanish has expanded her skill. Last year, after a week in Belize, she had made a comment that I think was telling. "At the beginning of the week, I couldn't understand any of the Spanish I heard, even after (then) four years of Spanish class. But I found by the end of the week that I learned to listen differently, and then I could understand what they were saying." Her philosophical momma quietly noted the integrative shift. This year, as she was returning home, someone beside her in line going through customs spoke to her in English. Starr replied, "I'm sorry, I didn't understand you; I've been speaking Spanish for a month!"

When she got home, she was saying how she would like to major in Romance languages, because they are all so similar to Spanish and to English. "You can just look at them and tell what they are saying." Later, I found her pondering in wonder a Chinese translation of J. K. Rowling's *Harry Potter* that my second daughter, Stacey, had recently brought back from Beijing. "When I look at this, I don't see in it anything that means anything at all," she said. She was contrasting it to how she glimpses meaning when she looks at Romance languages. I had had a similar feeling when I looked at that book: I felt as if I might as well be looking at a wall.

Not to leave my third daughter, Stephanie, out of the storytelling: When she was young enough to be buckled in a car seat, I remember her saying to me as we drove, "You know, when you know how to read, you can't not read. You can't not know that the stop sign says *stop*."

For each daughter, I have a photo I took of her as a child at the moment when, having taught her beginning phonetics, I put the simplest of books in her hands. Each face is registering a light bulb, "Oh! I see it!" moment of wonder and delight.

In light of the coherent pattern to which we have integrated, the particulars become clues, parts of the whole. They look at times completely different. They gain fresh function, appearance, and significance. When we achieve a fresh coherent pattern, it can transform both our world and our selves. Integration shifts the status of the clues, and that's what transforms them.

Chinese characters for me are simply that—Chinese characters. They have no meaning. Their strokes I cannot tell apart in any significant way. I can even stare very deliberately at each of the strokes, but I find it no more than an exercise in art appreciation. Suppose I showed you the Chinese copy of *Harry Potter*. Then I laid the English one beside it. If you're like me, the English words are transparent and powerful. They catapult you into reminiscences of middle school exploits at Hogwarts. This was the delightful experience of many young readers. It was Starr's experience when she found she could listen through the Spanish instead of to it.

Thus integration powerfully assigns fresh meaning to its parts. And it also changes the way they appear. Another thing that changes is the way the components feel to us. In the transforming feat, the clues come to feel lived—so many tools that extend our being. I no longer focus on the hammer's percussive impacts on the surfaces of my hand. I know it in its use, and my being engages the world at the outer reaches of my skilled efforts, in nails and drywall and remodeled bathrooms.

More than that, I myself am changed, for the clues that are transformed are in significant measure my self. Think simply of the statements that I take to be true. One set of statements gets superseded by another, often in a way that has powerful existential import. I was nine months pregnant with our second child. I woke suddenly in the wee hours of the morning. The statement I would have uttered, had I not been running to the bathroom, would have been "I'm having a gastrointestinal attack." It kept happening. It was two hours before it gradually began to dawn on me that it was happening *every five minutes!* I suddenly recognized a profounder pattern: I was going to have a baby—soon! My outlook was transformed, my course was altered, and my household was quickly galvanized into action!

■ Knowing Auto Mechanics and God: Transformed Clues, Transformed Knower

Admittedly, this transforming feature of the act of knowing is a little difficult to apply to knowing my auto mechanic, Jeff! I can't exactly say, "I'm a new woman!" because I know Jeff! I could say this about my experience of getting to know Jim, the man who became my husband. And it also aptly describes a person's conversion to following Christ.

The best "Oh! I see it!" moment in the Bible is the story of the disciples traveling on the road to Emmaus. Jesus, their leader and their hope for Israel, had been executed. He had been the one they thought was the Messiah, God's promised deliverer of their oppressed nation. No doubt Jesus' death had been profoundly upsetting, shaking them to the core of their being. They didn't know yet that Jesus had, in the last twenty-four hours, been raised from the dead!

As they were walking to Emmaus, a man they did not recognize joined them, and they proceeded to the town together. He asked what they were talking about. They were surprised that he had to ask; everybody in Jerusalem was talking about Jesus' death.

The man replied, "How foolish you are, and how slow of heart to believe all that the prophets have spoken! Did not the Messiah have to suffer these things and then enter his glory?" And he proceeded to explain to the disciples all that the Scriptures had said concerning the Messiah.

How strange it must have seemed to those disciples! Who was this man who knew Scripture better than they did, and who didn't seem to share their distress nor understand the events that provoked it? I surmise that this paradoxical state of affairs was tugging and poking at their thoughts, but they had yet to figure out its significance. At that point it was not yet apparent to them what the passage says was happening—that the man was telling them what Scripture said about *himself!*

There is, when you are doing the Magic Eye, a point in the struggle when some part of the picture starts to look intriguing or interesting. Something seems to be happening there. It catches your attention. But you can't tell its significance. What you are seeing makes sense as part of the eventually seen pattern of dolphins, but that is still mostly hidden, hidden enough that you don't yet know what's going on. I think this compares to the disciples' experience at this point. Something was wriggling, starting to happen. They sensed an as yet unidentified significance. And I have to say again, we know this experience because it is a regular feature of our day-to-day lives.

Why didn't they recognize him? I suggest that a big part of it was their working assumption that dead men don't rise to life again. It's not that they weighed this in their reasoning. It's that it never occurred to them that it might be otherwise. It would not have fit with their lived sense of rationality. And so their perception was blinded.

And then they encountered another wriggle of significance on the surface of their experience, this time a more telling one. The disciples invited the man to eat with them. The man broke bread and gave thanks . . . something they would have seen and heard and felt Jesus do innumerable times.

Can you put yourself in their sandals? It makes my spine tingle to think of it! Wave after wave of understanding broke over them: It was Jesus! Jesus was alive! Dead men do rise again—if they're divine! Jesus is the Son of God! The Scriptures were right—more right than we knew! Our confidence in him was better placed than we ever dreamed! Jesus is the answer to something far worse than the Romans; he's the answer to sin and death! He is the first taste of God's restoration of all things! Think of the possibilities! We shall be utterly saved! Final victory is assured!

The particular features of their world, the Word, and themselves were radically transformed. Think how now they would view Jesus' death, his claims, his actions. They would now compose an almost entirely different, far grander picture. Think how it would have transformed their view of Old Testament prophecy. "Fulfilled" is far too weak a word; "exploded" comes closer. Jesus didn't merely confirm predictions and explain puzzles; he transformed them. They must have remembered Jesus saying, in a rather understated way: "One greater than Solomon is here." The tables had been radically turned.

The Bible says that when Jesus broke the bread, the disciples' eyes were opened and they recognized him. After Jesus had gone, they asked each other, "Were not our hearts burning within us while he talked with us on the road and opened the Scriptures to us?" It's as if their bodies were resonating to Jesus' identity before their minds had grasped it. And think how it would have felt to realize that the one who had been expounding the Old Testament to you was the one who had written it!

In my second favorite "Oh! I see it!" moment—well, three days—of the Bible, the Christian-hater Saul was tracking Christians from Jerusalem to Damascus to persecute them. This zealous Jew of Jews was taking it upon himself to snuff out this upstart and dangerous movement. While Saul was on the road, Jesus somehow made himself known to Saul. A sudden light from heaven flashed around the startled man. He fell to the ground and heard a voice say to him, "Saul, Saul, why do you persecute me?" When Saul asked, "Who are you, Lord?" the voice said, "I am Jesus, whom you are persecuting. Now get up and go into the city, and you will be told what you must do."

Blinded by the encounter, Saul was led to Damascus. The Scriptures say that for three days he was blind and did not eat or drink anything.

What do you think was going through Saul's mind during those three days? I suggest that, like the disciples in Emmaus, wave after wave of understanding was breaking over him. Think of it: this man knew the Old Testament Scriptures backwards and forwards. He didn't know Jesus—or rather, he hadn't believed that Jesus was the one of whom the Law and the Prophets testify. And Jesus had been executed. He believed that the disciples had trumped up the stories of Jesus' resurrection. Then a living Jesus addressed Saul out of what could only be a divine self-revelation. Saul didn't have an as yet unrecognized Jesus alongside him to go over the Scriptures with him. He didn't need it. I suggest that for those three cataclysmic days Saul's mind and heart raced through the Scriptures he knew by heart, tracing over ground once so familiar with freshly opened eyes of insight, seeing a new and transforming coherence in them that now anchored in Jesus, God's "one who was to come."

The features of his Word, his world, and his entire being gained in those three days a fresh, transforming meaning. Jesus was no longer who he had thought he was; the Scripture no longer said what he had thought it said; and Saul himself was no longer, and never could again be, the man he had once

111

been. God was setting apart his last apostle, Paul, to take the good news of Jesus Christ beyond the expected boundaries to unheard-of and positively scandalous regions beyond: to the Gentiles.

Other conversion experiences in the Bible show the same thing: The integrative act of knowing transforms the look and feel of the features of our world, our word, and ourselves on which we rely as we focus on a fresh pattern. Jesus tells a fishless Peter to drop the fishing nets another time. The net starts to break under the sudden load of scores of flopping sea creatures. Peter cries to Jesus, "Go away from me, I am a sinful man!" A startling conclusion, indicative of a transformed outlook. Thomas sees and feels the spike and spear wounds in the risen Jesus' hands and side and cries to Jesus, "My Lord and my God!" I can't think of words big enough to describe the depth and complexity of his emotion at that moment. Another startling conclusion that reveals just how far reaching the transformation of his outlook has been.

If you are a believer, your conversion may have felt to you like this. Everything in your life and your world gained fresh significance. The words that you struggled to grasp went from walls to windows as you met Jesus. For the believer, a moment of profound worship is like this also, whenever we contemplate afresh just who it is we know, and just what he has done. Worship regularly transforms us and our world.

In this respect, perhaps, knowing our auto mechanic and knowing God seem to differ. But this difference strengthens rather than weakens the case for knowing God being like ordinary knowing. We have discussed other very human experiences that evidence this transforming of the features of our lives. Perhaps learning to read isn't as grand a transformation as recognizing the Messiah, and perhaps banking on this auto mechanic as opposed to that one isn't as life-changing as learning to read. But these acts of knowing share the same dynamic, and that is my point. Recognizing the Messiah is the sort of act of knowing that we would expect to transform every dimension of life, where relying on a certain auto mechanic may not be. But this is the kind of variation that characterizes acts of knowing. It confirms that knowing God falls right in there with other bona fide specimens of knowing.

For Further Thought and Discussion

Find examples of personal transformation. Can you think of some moments of discovery or learning that were personally transformational? Describe one or more of these.

Consider the act of knowing. Why might it be surprising to think that knowing changes the knower?

Consider Christianity. For people who have become Christians, personal transformation, their own and others', seems to be a telling confirmation of the truth of the claims they have embraced. Given that the thing being known is God (as opposed, say, to an auto mechanic), is it reasonable to expect significant personal transformation? Is it reasonable to expect that a person who comes to know God would experience little transformation?

PART IV

. . . To Focus on a Coherent Pattern and Submit to Its Reality

Knowing
is the responsible human struggle
to rely on clues
to focus on a coherent pattern
and submit to its reality.

15

Patterns—the Surprising Fruit of Our Struggle

Coherent Centers of Meaning and Agency

Knowing is the human act of making sense of experience, connecting the dots. It is shaping a plethora of details in and around us, alongside us and ahead of us, in pursuit of a pattern. We access the pattern by struggling to look through the details to a farther focus. A successful effort transforms the clues we rely on. We've talked about that actual struggle to integrate to a focus, and we've talked about the clues on which we rely subsidiarily both before and then within the focus. In doing this, we already have said a lot about foci. Thinking about foci per se should consolidate the gains of our learning.

Having integrated the features of our Magic Eye experience to their focus, we see three-dimensional dolphins swimming in an underwater wonderland. An outline emerges, a meaningful something. It is coherent in the sense that the once unrelated pieces of it now stick together in a meaningful, identifiable center.

In philosophical discussions, that word "coherence" has often been used to describe a set of statements that are mutually consistent with each other. Coherence typically means that all the statements can be true at the same time. When

I use the word, however, I have something more substantial, something richer and "stickier" in mind. To use an analogy: contrast flour "cohering" by dint of sharing the same space in a dry measuring cup with flour "cohering" in a lump of yeasty, rising dough. The coherence I have in mind has an inescapable center, an identifiable agent of future activity. (Think of a person you know well as being such a coherent center.) Now, probably you can articulate a set of statements that describe this coherent center and its place in the world. But you probably also sense that their two-dimensional consistency is eclipsed by a profundity, a unity, and even a beauty beyond the bare statements, a farther center from which the statements derive their significance.

Our conviction of the rightness of our pattern is not merely a result of our running it by some test of verbal consistency. The thing is there. It's as if the thing is staring sarcastically down at us, as a 300-pound defensive tackle might, as it says to us, "You want *me* to take a coherence test?" Somehow any such test is superseded. Such a test isn't useless. It's that it is only two-dimensional. In our accessing a focal pattern we encounter a three-dimensionality, only some of which we capture in words, but some of the rest of which we nevertheless surmise to be there. As you already know, we need not think that this sensing is mystical. It is just the skilled, felt sense of the real that extends the frontiers of our bodily, lived awareness. We sense the three-dimensionality of our pattern as we sense our balance on a bike, or the proper consistency of bread dough.

Philosophers have often spoken of consistency, simplicity, beauty, and fruitfulness as criteria that confirm the effectiveness of our verbal claims. Most of these philosophers have been working from within a model of knowledge that equates knowledge with statements and justification with exhaustive verbal proof. And as such, the terms have been a bit problematic. For, when applied to discoveries such as the heliocentric solar system or relativity, the terms turn out to be informed with meaning from the other end, so to speak. The scientific community comes to sense the consistency and simplicity and beauty and fruitfulness of the pattern, but were you to wield the criteria as an outside observer, you might not automatically conclude that the theory of relativity is beautiful, or simple. And for the discoverers, it's too early to confirm that it's fruitful.

Successful focal patterns are simple and beautiful and consistent and fruitful. But the characteristics are shaped and actualized by the focus, and not vice versa. A focus is beautiful and unified because it's a focus; it's not a focus because it is beautiful and unified. It is possible for something to be both complex and simple, profound in its unity, fruitful not only in confirming what we already know but fruitful in prospects, only if it is there. Far from determining it by means of such assessments, we defer to it in such assessments. This is all to say that simplicity, beauty, and other such criteria function as all clues do in pursuit of a focus: we struggle to get inside their meaning as they bear on the focus that we grope toward. The focus, once achieved, infuses transforming meaning retroactively into the very things we navigate by seeking to understand.

Our house borders a wooded area that shelters an array of interesting wildlife. Soon after we moved here, my little girls excitedly summoned me to look at what they had encountered on one of the paths. I ran to look and saw nothing—at first. The girls weren't telling me what I was looking for, either. I was struggling to integrate to some sort of pattern. Only after some time did I see the copperhead that was sitting there looking back at me!

We had just learned at a nearby nature center that copperhead snakes are identifiable by the "Hershey Kisses" that mark their backs. (Note the role of an authoritative guide in teaching us to notice, and to see what is there.) This thing had a beautiful set of Hershey Kisses; there was no doubt what it was. When I saw it, even as I was noting the Kisses, I was seeing a snake. It was a coherent center of meaning, an agent with initiative. Now, copperheads are one of two poisonous snakes in Missouri—we learned that at the nature center, too. I was not exactly thinking of the truth of statements at that moment, nor of criteria of beauty and simplicity and consistency and fruitfulness! I was getting ready to grab my children! You can imagine how the fear and excitement felt, rising within me! This mom launched into a lecture to her daughters about watching every step they took in the woods. Integration to the outline of a copperhead on a woodland path did, and was, more than could be exhaustively represented by a set of statements. It involved a real me in a real world.

No matter how difficult the struggle to achieve a focus, once you get to the focus, as we say, it's no longer about you—as they say. It's about the focus. Forget your struggle to see the copperhead; deal with the copperhead. Childbirth is a great example: it's mom who undergoes the struggle of birth. But every birthday thereafter, it's the child who gets the party!! Nor do parents typically feel this inequity, for the reality of their child makes the whole struggle worthwhile.

You and I do not even see the things that as yet have not been the focus of our integrative effort, even though they are there under our noses. I remember a recent service call from a pest exterminator. We had asked him to check our house for termites. When I first greeted him at the door, he confronted me: "Do you know that your house has been treated for termites before?" (An epistemic question! And note the exterminator's role as authoritative word!) My jaw dropped and my eyes widened. "How do you know that?" I asked. (Another epistemic question—life is brimming with them!) He pointed to some tiny circular cement patches on the step at our feet, holes drilled and patched, he said, in the course of termite treatment. Up to that moment, I had never seen them, though I have swept the step hundreds of times! But having seen them, they are now undeniably there. (And, I hope, the termites are not!)

These examples and the many experiences of our lives show that our successful integration to a focus is a seeing what is there. It very often is the case that in the seeing or in subsequent reflection, our mouths are opened and we put words on what we see and criteria to which the experience conforms. But the naming or describing is not all there is to the event. The coherence of the pattern is "stickier," more substantial than a mere set of consistent statements of description. If in our pattern making we are seeing what is there, then our pattern making is never merely pattern making. It's more like self-transformation through pattern making. Maybe we start it, but then the tables turn. The power of the pattern, we will see, is that it mediates to us the world, and thus it properly summons us to submission. You don't argue with copperheads and exterminators.

■ Interpreting the Gaps

Another thing that shows the three-dimensionality of our achieved focus is what we do, in the moment of integration, with the gaps. When the knower moves in his or her struggle from dissociated particulars to integrated coherent pattern, what once looked like empty spaces gets reinterpreted as hiddennesses. What I mean by a hiddenness is a space to which we assign the meaning of being there, but around the corner, so to speak. It is a horizon of the object, such that if this object is the thing I now take it to be, of course I can't see that side of it at the moment.

The baby who learns to interpret the cloth over his or her father's face not as eliminating but rather as hiding the father is now ready to play peek-a-boo. This is an integrative achievement that almost every parent can mark. For prior to that time, with the onset of the handkerchief, the baby would just look elsewhere. After the new focus, the baby delightedly waits for Daddy to reappear, or peeks around the handkerchief. In the fresh focus, the baby has reinterpreted the gaps as hiddennesses fraught with just the sort of meaning you would expect, given the integrity of the focus.

We look at a sliver of moon and surmise that we're seeing part of an orb, not all of a crescent. Part of an orb, not all of a crescent! The crucial difference is that we see the empty space as something hidden. Quite literally, in the case of the moon, we trace an outline, and at the point of the gap in the outline, we say the pattern is there, but hidden. And this is what you would expect from a three-dimensional orb only one of whose sides is reflecting the light of the sun.

To see that an empty space is really a hidden portion is to give meaning to that space in light of the larger pattern. Our coherences have gaps, but the gaps, once they are embedded in the coherences, eloquently testify to the profound three-dimensionality, the coherent unity of our pattern, a center of agency that now responds to us.

Even the simplest act of perception involves our assigning such significance to hiddennesses. This is what visual perspective, and foreshortening, is all about. My daughter recently photographed a toddler sitting on her bed. In the photo, the baby's head is about an inch from top to bottom; his body is less than an inch! What I see is that the photographer was shooting down at the baby. I interpret the relative sizes in light of my lived grasp of proportion.

At the moment I sit, with my laptop, on our deck. You can tell it's August by the peculiar noise in the hickory trees and the whitish bits falling out of them. Is the tree snowing? No, I know squirrels are doggedly chomping on every hickory nut they can get their paws on. The significance I attribute to the hiddenness makes the coherent pattern what it is.

The saddest moment in the movie *Ben Hur* is the moment when Judah Ben Hur's mother and sister are discovered in the deepest, most hideous dungeon. The door has not been opened for years. But the guard knows they are alive. He kicks a grimy little trap door open with his foot. "I know they're alive," he says. "The food disappears." The guard gives a certain significance of hiddenness to a gap in the process of shaping a coherent pattern. Both the happy and the horrible in our knowing show a pattern with meaningful hiddennesses. In every act of knowing we move to a focal pattern that extends beyond the initially known to give meaning to the gaps.

The coherence of a good pattern is more than a set of consistent statements. It is more than wooden or two-dimensional. The focus assigns fresh meaning to simplicity and beauty and fruitfulness and consistency. Having struggled to integrate to a focus, we find the focus is a coherent center. The focus is in the driver's seat; fasten your seatbelts!

121

◼ Knowing Auto Mechanics and God: Coherent Centers Fraught with Significance

When it comes to knowing my auto mechanic, I could describe what I know as "Jeff is a good, reliable, trustworthy auto mechanic." But what I know is the thing, the auto mechanic, the pattern that is there, a center of identity, meaning, and, thankfully, reliable agency. I hardly consider the fact that I rarely see him. Of course I don't see him—he's nice enough to get my car picked up from the seminary. The hiddenness confirms his greatness.

When it comes to knowing God, I describe what I know as "I believe in God, the Father Almighty," using the words of the Apostles' Creed, and more broadly of Scripture itself. But what I know is a person, the pattern that is there as a center of identity, meaning, and, thankfully, reliable agency. I hardly consider the fact that I rarely see him. Of course I don't see him. God "lives in unapproachable light," the apostle Paul says indicating God's power and goodness. Jesus told his disciples, "I am going [to my Father's house] to prepare a place for you. . . . I will come back and take you to be with me." Of course I don't see him now. The hiddenness confirms his greatness.

In making sense of God, people come up against some gaps that trouble them. Why doesn't God punish evildoers immediately? If God is who he says he is, why do some people get away with evil things? Plus, God said he would come. Where is he? The biblical writers dealt with these questions, and in their responses, they assigned meaning to the gaps in the pattern. God has allowed you to continue in your rebellion, Paul says, not because he is a wimp (I paraphrase) but because he shows a kindness that should lead you to repentance. Why has he not come? Peter says that he is being patient with you, not wanting anyone to perish, but wanting everyone to come to repentance. But the day of the Lord will come, he says. A misinterpretation of this gap will be your eternal ruin.

And consider here the profundity of the pattern! The pattern of God's ways and words stretches to the very edges of my life experience and greets me each new day with fresh installments. The grand drama of redemption recorded in Scripture lends meaning to my human experience. In light of it I recognize my dignity as a human, the inherent worth of my efforts in this world, and the longing for glory and restoration that my pain and brokenness cry out for. Plus, integrating to the pattern of the God of Scripture takes "coherent center of agency" to a new level! It's far beyond the 300-pound defensive tackle. It's also far beyond knowing my auto mechanic. The focus has turned the tables on me on a cosmic scale.

Acts of knowing involve us in shaping coherent patterns that connect the dots of our experience, interpreting the gaps as meaningful hiddennesses and horizons of possibility. While achieving the focus takes my active effort, the pattern's three-dimensionality indicates the presence of a center that then shapes my own sense of its consistency. While knowing God in this respect outdistances knowing an auto mechanic, do not both acts display this feature?

For Further Thought and Discussion

Find personal examples. Can you think of examples in which you have achieved a focal pattern you felt was profound? Remember that all acts of learning and discovery involve struggling to shape patterns, to make sense of experience. Describe your feelings about the pattern. What adjectives convey your assessment of the pattern? In what ways did you feel that the pattern you had shaped began to shape you?

Gauge the relative profundity of patterns. Can you think of experiences in which you have sensed a shallowness of your focal pattern? How do we employ this criterion when we assess people, and when we assess literary works?

Consider the patterns of your life. Do you see patterns and significances in your own life as a whole? Does the record of God's work in the world, recorded in the Bible, shape your personal pattern? Should it? Do the patterns in your life point in another direction? Express some of your thoughts about this.

16

Contact with Reality

What Makes Us Think
We've Accessed the World

You may remember that one of the burning questions that propelled me into a philosophical search was, How can I know that there is a world out there? You can see that this is obviously related to the other burning question I had: How can I know that God is out there? When I learned about the model of knowing that I am developing in this book, I found it intriguing partly because it seemed to hold a possible answer to what had felt like an unanswerable question about knowing the world. That's what I am excited to tell you about in this chapter.

So the question is, In our knowing, do we access a real, external world, a world that exists independently of my knowing it? And if so, how would I ever know? My answer to these questions grows out of the things I have been saying about the coherent pattern that emerges from the knowing agent's integrative act. I want to draw out more boldly some of the things I hinted at in the last chapter.

On the traditional model of knowledge, what we know is facts or statements that describe states of affairs. "It is raining." "Jim is at the store." "My car needs new struts." What would make these statements "knowledge," it was thought by many people, would be for them to be true (How can they be knowledge if they're not true?), and for the person affirming these claims to have good reason for doing so (If we were just guessing and only accidentally right, how could we consider them to be knowledge?). But the rub that I felt, as I'm sure everybody did, is this: How *do* you tell if they are *true?* If knowledge is limited to statements, by definition how can you have a "knowledge" of whether the statements match the world? You can't seem to get outside of your words. They imprison you, stand between you and the very thing you are concerned to know. This is tremendously frustrating, even agonizing.

The intriguing, hope-giving anomaly in this scenario is that knowing *happens.* Something inside me quietly beat this counterpoint all through my doubt. It made me feel sheepish for having the question. But it also indicated that perhaps the question was faulty, or the model of knowledge that perpetrated it.

The new model, of knowing as relying on subsidiaries to shape patterns, has shown already that there is and must be more to knowledge than words, or we would never even be capable of the words. There must be features of our knowing that we can't put into words. In the previous chapters, we have learned to recognize some of these inarticulable features: the skilled human effort, an effort that involves a risky extending of ourselves; an active reassigning of significance that, at the time of the effort, lacks explicit justification; a relying on clues that we can't specify, or if we can, it is our embodying them, not our verbal description of them, that moves us forward. Our truth claims crest these inarticulate layers; they exist by virtue of their roots in human commitment.

Do all these very human, active contributions to the act of knowing only add to the baggage that hinders us from comparing our truth claims to the world? How, especially with my personal involvement, would I ever know the world all by itself, apart from my shaping of the world? How does this help me to know that there is a world out there apart from my knowing it? How can I know if my words connect with reality, or bar me from reality? How can I be sure there is even a reality to be known? Perhaps my patterns are all there is to it.

We need to reinterpret this personal human effort, not as the barrier that prevents knowing but as the situatedness in the world that just is our strategic access to it. We don't need a beachhead; we already are one. And our situated efforts then get repaid in the telltale dividends of the real.

125

■ The Profundity of the Pattern

We need to go back and think through what happens when we integrate from clues to focus. What is it that gives us the "Oh! I see it!" feeling—the feeling that something is there, was there, waiting to be discovered, will be there when we return to it? Why do we feel that our focal pattern is a discovery, not an invention?

Two accompanying experiences make us feel this way. The first is our sense of the richness, the profundity, of the pattern. If we see dolphins, we know we've done it right. The pattern is that much grander than the clues on which it relies.

Patterns more than make sense of the clues—those in the world, those in our bodies, and those in the directions, those we can name and those we can't. The pattern unites and transforms them into a fresh center, in light of which the clues gain profounder meaning. The pattern evokes uncanny harmonies and resonances between things that once appeared disparate. The gaps become meaningful hiddennesses. There's just more going on than seems accounted for by what you are able to describe of the process and the pattern. And since some of these clues were deep in our body, our whole felt sense of the thing changes too.

I have just said nothing new about the epistemic act. I have only added the claim that the effect of undergoing the experience we have been talking about is to make us feel that we have in the process contacted reality, bumped into, accessed, something real.

A cryptogram is a message encoded by systemically substituting one letter for another letter. Solving it requires you to look for any possible clues concerning what letter might be standing for what letter, and then risking a shot. Suppose, for example, that the cryptogram has a one-letter word in it. It's obvious that that letter is either *A* or *I*. But then you have to choose to try one, and you fill it in for every occurrence of the letter in question. Navigating in this way, eventually you come to a point where you are uncovering meaningful words and phrases. Your success tells you that you are uncovering the true message. Nobody seriously considers that there might be more than one answer. Meaningful words and phrases are far too profound a pattern not to be a reality. The richness of the pattern testifies to its reality.

In the *Star Wars* movies, at the end of Episode 6 (the third movie), Luke, Leia, Han, and the audience find out that Luke and Leia are siblings. In light of this new revelation, the connectedness that Luke and Leia had evidenced and felt makes perfect and profound sense. The fresh focal pattern, "Luke and

Leia are twins," more than makes sense of what they knew. It transforms it, gives fresh meaning, evokes a body sense that outruns words. It's as much what we can't put into words as what we can put into words that testifies to the rightness of the pattern. It is the profundity of the pattern that testifies to us that we have not merely shaped a pattern, but that in doing so we have also unlocked the world.

■ Unspecifiable Future Prospects

When we experience the profundity of our focal pattern, we have the sense that we have contacted the real. What we experience is its transforming of the very features of our world, our bodies, and our guides, on which we relied in its pursuit. A second accompanying experience also confirms the reality of our pattern. We sense another range of profundity, but where the other grew out of our past, this second one grows into our future.

In the moment of a profound integration, we experience a sense of the future possibilities, prospects, horizons of the thing we have encountered. There are sides we cannot currently see, behaviors we suspect but could never predict, implications only some of which we can reason out, but which in their incompleteness may lead us to uncover new and transforming dimensions. We could in no way exhaustively list those possibilities. We can't even name them all. Yet they in their unnameableness confirm the rightness of our integration. This sense of possibilities furnishes us with a second indicator that we have contacted the real.

It's simply a lovely moment when the smile of understanding spreads slowly across Han's face. "Luke and Leia are twins!" What a nice way to solve a love triangle! Leia is free to care for both men, and each man is free to care for her in a really special, different way. Han has fresh hope of love with Leia. Suddenly the way before him is wonderfully clear, and the future is bright with possibilities. Does it hold marriage to this princess of his dreams? Does it solidify his solidarity with his friend, Luke? Is it the end of his financial trouble? Will Luke and Leia's blended strength, teamed with Han's scrappy aid, together conquer the dark forces for good? There are definitely tantalizing horizons to explore. There is no way of telling exactly what will happen, but those delicious possibilities confirm the reality of the claim that Luke and Leia are twins.

Is it only movie viewers that get excited about possibilities? Of course not. I remember the moment that the man whom I eventually married caught my attention in more than a superficial way. I had the feeling of looking down a well, and I couldn't see the bottom. I was sensing that there was much more to this man that was there to explore, and I wanted to explore it.

Many years ago, at the time when I was first thinking and writing about this approach to knowledge, I viewed a television documentary that featured some marine biologists and their discovery of vents on the ocean floor. The interviewed biologists were jubilant. "This is the discovery of the century!" one exclaimed. "The possible implications of it are profound, more than we are able to tell." Humans, especially those skilled with respect to the discipline in question, sense and navigate forward guided by an unspecifiable sense of future possibilities.

In a recent book on love, philosopher Caroline Simon offers a fresh definition of the perennially puzzling term. Love, she proposes, is imagining someone's destiny. It is to be distinguished from fiction-making, in that fiction-making falsely represents someone's destiny. Love is imagining someone's destiny truly.

The one who loves sees truly the possibilities of the beloved. This formula profoundly challenges the traditional model of knowledge! It involves sensing future possibilities, and sensing them truly, even when you can't articulate them. It involves seeing the man or woman you love as he or she is now in light of a destiny that will be the developed expression of all that is best in him or her. A good friend is one who knows you *and* believes in you, as we say. A good friend weighs your day-to-day behavior with a view to your true destiny in a way that we cannot even do for ourselves at times.

By contrast, Caroline Simon offers the sad example of Dorothea Brooke, in George Eliot's *Middlemarch*, who reads into Mr. Casaubon's behavior qualities of her own liking, only to discover her own fiction-making after she marries him. Even if you are dealing in possibilities, we can and must talk about *truth:* you can be wrong even as you can be right.

Sense perception is no different from knowing persons. Remember the copperhead? When I finally saw the thing, a pattern emerged from a background. I could have pointed to the surface features of my world and labeled them: "This is snake; this is leafy woodland floor." But there were also hidden horizons I surmised tacitly to be there. Its three-dimensionality suggested an underside and innards. I had to think about fangs and venom. There were the possible outcomes of a copperhead bite. And there were the prospects of the event for parenting three little girls living on the verge of a woods. One could consider copperhead behavior and copperhead habitat. My sense of this copperhead's reality rode to me on the wave of his possibilities. The same is true of my sense of the reality of the woods. I expected unexpected eventualities.

The future possibilities are indeterminate—we can't say at the moment exactly what they are. They do surprise us, and thus we could never predict them in an exhaustive way. The human knower cannot therefore totally determine his or her "own" truth. For too much of it is future, and we are always surprised.

There simply has to be another player in the knowing game, another variable in the formula. The profounder the reality of the thing with which we play, the vaster the possibilities and occasions for surprise.

It's our sense of what we don't know about the thing in question, as much as what we do know about it, that confirms its reality. But I speak misleadingly, for the sake of effect. For "what we don't know" refers to what is hidden. It's not that ignorance or bare, senseless gaps confirm reality. It is hiddenness fraught with meaning, a knowing that can't be expressed in words because it is not yet, that strengthens our conviction that the pattern is no mere mental invention, but real.

But these unspecifiable prospects, while surprising, are nevertheless profoundly consistent with the character of the real thing in question. Maybe you couldn't have predicted some of the things that happen, but once they happen, you can see how very consistent the outcomes are with the character of the thing you know. It surprised me that a copperhead was sighted twenty feet behind my house. But it was very like a living Missouri woods to produce one. It gave me a greater respect for the reality of the woods behind my house and the prospect of living on the verge of them.

You never know a person exhaustively enough to stop being surprised by some things he or she does. I can remember my aunt saying, "I never could have anticipated what your uncle would be like with his grandchildren." Yet when someone you know surprises you, it is often the case later that you find yourself saying, "How very like them!"

Now, we can imagine a different kind of surprise that *would* obliterate our sense of the reality of a thing. It would be an irrational or inconsistent surprise, as opposed to a transformingly, profoundly consistent one. If Daddy really did disappear when the handkerchief moves in between, Baby would end up with a different notion of Daddy's reality, one in which, perhaps, "Daddy" did not name a real thing. Maybe he would be part of the random background of the handkerchief. This distinction, between profoundly consistent surprises and irrational ones, is one that we understand experientially.

If as we have said a pattern turns gaps into hiddennesses, we can say that this sense that we have, at the moment of integration, of hints of unsayable, future, surprising confirmations of the pattern is just another sort of gap-turned-hiddenness. Unlike surface or body features, however, it is located in *time*. It is

129

a making meaningful of the hiddenness of the future. Our sense of possibilities is thus of a piece with the integrative pattern. We have already said that the act of knowing vectors us through time. But now we see that the pattern itself is embedded in time. Thus, this second indicator of contact with reality, our sense of the future possibilities of the pattern, is the temporal cousin of the first, our sense of the profundity of the pattern.

Nowadays we have a wonderfully evocative term for a pattern embedded in time: we call it "story." Stories unfold. We can tell the difference between a good story and a bad story as we assess the relative richness and coherence of its possibilities. And we know very well what it is like to be in the middle of a story, to have and to be drawn on by the sense of unforeseeable implications. Our sense of the pattern's future hiddenness testifies to us of its reality.

And we as humans are beings who live toward the future. To be human is to anticipate, to hope, to value in light of prospects. To use a theological word— we are eschatological beings. This is one reason why our misperceptions about knowledge have been so tragic. It is also why it is contrary to humanness to surrender the hope of truth.

■ Telltale Features of the Real

Why does profundity of this more-than-articulable sort testify to contact with the real? Because it is just the sort of thing you would expect from anything real. There is no way that anybody can stand outside of our body- and time-bound efforts and proclaim without reference to them that reality has certain characteristics. But we don't need to. We all have a lifetime of experiences of the real as that which is profoundly rich and inexhaustive even as it is coherent. We navigate continually in light of this tacit understanding.

Consider the two movies, *The Truman Show* and *A Beautiful Mind*. In each, the main character eventually recognizes the wooden two-dimensionality of that which he has been led to believe is real, and he opts for something he believes to be more real. It can be done. Humans do it all the time. Of course we can be mistaken. Of course it is at times hard to improve our grasp on the real, but each of us is a tapestry of a good number of such successes.

In recent years I have worked for an organization that came into existence because of a generous grant from the Lilly Foundation. My task has been to fulfill Lilly's stipulation that we continuously articulate our vision, develop programs that justifiably will enable us to fulfill our vision, and assess and record our progress. Before I had heard the people at Lilly express what they wanted to see in writing, I would have thought that they wanted to receive documentation that we fulfilled the goals that we set about pursuing. But I found that they were more interested in "surprising outcomes" and "significant learnings." It was not as important and valuable that we confirmed our original proposals as that we allowed them to be shaped by significant surprises along the way. It wasn't that Lilly didn't care if we had any vision at all, or that we might reverse course totally.

Last year our organization experienced a huge Lilly-style surprising outcome. If we had assessed it as a failure to conform to our original plan, we would have not valued it aright, and we would have missed out on something bigger. What this experience felt like to us was that our vision's reality was confirmed. It had a life of its own, and we were coming to view it as an organism with a character that we had come to recognize. I think the people at Lilly understand that the reality of a vision is confirmed by surprising, transformingly consistent, future manifestations.

Our sense of the possibilities of our pattern confirm to us that in it we have contacted the real.

How do my words connect to reality? I integrate to them, and I integrate through them to grasp an aspect of the real. Let's consider the statement "There is a copperhead in the woods." The statement has its roots in the clues of the Meek girls' world: the word of the naturalist at the center, the distinctive pattern on the path, and the visual struggle it takes to achieve it. But the effort of knowing doesn't just stop there. For the words point beyond themselves to the greater focus: the snake itself. Nor do the words exhaust the reality. Heaven forfend—there may be a colony of them. Or maybe this guy wandered unusually far away from his home. I don't know how many copperheads my girls are liable to encounter. I wonder about how good their eyes are, and whether they'll remember my warning to be careful. I navigate in light of the possibilities. My actions unfold in response, and the world responds to my initiatives with initiatives of its own.

That day years ago the copperhead and I regarded each other for some minutes. We related to each other as agent to agent, each capable of surprising future manifestations, to whom the other must defer. I won the staring contest: he slid silently off the path. We all were shaped by that moment: we keep our eyes open in the woods, not just out of caution, but tantalized by the prospect of other sightings.

We live as centers of meaning and character in a world of such centers. There are always things that a copperhead is and things that he isn't, things he does that grow out of his profoundly coherent character, things he does to engage

131

us. And there are always surprising yet distinctly copperhead possibilities. We rightly surmise that he is something there.

■ Knowing Auto Mechanics and God: Profound Patterns, Indeterminate Prospects

Jeff is an auto mechanic with definite possibilities. My relying on him just means that I expect him to manifest himself in Jeff-like, car-healthy ways indefinitely in the future. I can't in any way specify at the moment exactly the form our future exchanges will take. I hope he won't have to send a tow truck to collect my old Taurus and me from the side of the road. But he might. I hope he won't have to fix my air conditioner again. But he might. I expect that he'll give me conscientious care and wise guidance. I can't tell you exactly what he'll have to care for or advise me on.

I can remember when I first heard that he had bought a gas station. He would no longer be working out of his parents' garage. My sense of the legitimacy and permanence—the reality—of his operation expanded. I surmised a solidity to his efforts that had been lacking when I knew he was working out of his parents' garage. I anticipated a broader range of future manifestations. But I couldn't have stipulated those manifestations.

My knowing of Jeff is a living, unfolding story. I can in no way predict the ending, or even the next chapter, and for just this reason I sense his reality, and the future draws me on.

Jeff is more than my mental construct. Jeff is there. My words grasp an aspect of reality. But only an aspect: there is much I don't know about Jeff, my car, and my future.

How do I know that God exists? We have already talked of the clues of my world and of my body and of the Word from which I integrate to a coherent pattern. But future possibilities testify to his reality, also. In fact, the possibilities of Jesus' claims make his reality the profoundest of all (which fits with his being God!). Each day that comes to me brings more events that have occurred in his world. Each discovery I make introduces me to sides of his creativity and wisdom and plan that I anticipated but nevertheless surprise me. Each person that I come to know offers fresh glimpses of his glory and his mercy. Each broken feature of the world and of my life that I encounter cries out for him to right it. Each "not the way it is supposed to be" points to one who will resolve it.

When the risen Jesus ascended into the clouds, he promised that he will return. But not only do we have his explicit promise. We have everything about God's character and his claims that point to his final victorious return. Yahweh, he teaches us about himself, is not like any other professed gods; he alone is the God who comes to his people.

We hear repeatedly in the Old Testament stories of his coming to his people—coming with deliverance, forgiveness, and righteous rule. Each part of the drama teaches us to expect and long for his final and climactic coming. Every fiber of our broken being groans for his coming, when all wrongs will be put right and all brokenness restored. Every literary story points to his archetypal story; every vernal rebirth to his archetypal restoration in progress. C. S. Lewis says that the Christian should say, "Jesus Christ was raised from the dead," the way we would say, "I saw a crocus yesterday." The last spring of the ages is imminent. It is only a matter of time.

To know him is to know that the God of the Bible is like this. To know God is to know the climax of history. To know God is to sense possibilities of future manifestations on the grandest of scales.

And the profundity of the pattern disposes me to believe Scripture's God is real. This is hardly a wooden construction—contrast the prophet Isaiah's sarcastic mirth about wooden idols: a man takes half a tree trunk and makes an idol; the other half he burns as firewood! Contrast the God of Israel, Isaiah says, Yahweh who has made all things, and who redeems his people! To glimpse the pattern is to be inclined to deem it real.

My knowing of God is a living, unfolding story. I cannot exhaustively articulate the ending, or even the next chapter, and for just this reason I sense his reality, and the future draws me on. Knowing anything involves entrusting oneself to the future, not fully specifiable, possibilities of the thing in question.

For Further Thought and Discussion

Consider what's real. Make a list of a few things you think are real or statements you take to be true. Include at least one tangible object, one true statement, and one person.

- Pretend you have a "possibilities meter" that gives readings from 0 to 100 to indicate the range of the item's hidden sides and future possibilities, or the richness of your sense of these possibilities. How does each of your examples score? Explain the variation in numbers.

133

- For each item on your list, name some of the horizons and possibilities that you can surmise are there.
- Is there a correlation between a higher number on the possibilities meter and your excitement about and interest in the object or statement?

Consider the movies. Both *The Truman Show* and *A Beautiful Mind* chronicle a person struggling to sort out reality from fake reality. If you've seen either of these lately, describe some of the clues that enable the main characters to do this.

Gauge your hope. As a result of what you have read, do you feel greater hope about contacting the real in your knowing? Why or why not? How does your level of hope play into any questions you have about knowing God?

17

Truth: Contact,
Not Correspondence;
Confidence, Not Certainty

Contrasting Two Models of Knowledge

Our integrative acts of knowing contact reality. We can tell that our patterns and our statements contact the real because we experience the profundity of our pattern and the richness of its prospects. In light of all this, how do we go on to speak of truth?

A common way that we used to speak of truth is to say that true statements correspond to reality. We had in mind a picturing or matching of word and object. Correspondence required precise representation. While this is a notion that in an informal way expresses our sense of truth, it becomes problematic when asked to bear the weight of formal analysis. The whole enterprise comes under fire: How could you ever jump outside yourself to assess objectively whether your statements match the world? And, short of that, how can we possibly measure the truth of our statements? Perhaps we must replace the notion of truth with consistency of statements, or some notion of effectiveness.

Understanding the beyond-words dimensions of human knowing, including our sense of contacting the real, enables us to speak of truth. I think we can replace the notion of *correspondence* with the notion of *contact*.

If it were possible for a statement to correspond to reality in a rigidly formal sense, it would have to exhaust that reality in its verbal description. If our acts of knowing include dimensions that defy verbalization, including future prospects, not only is it impossible for our statements to exhaust the reality they contact, but if they did, it wouldn't be reality that we had contacted. Exhaustive lucidity is sterile. Correspondence, in this sense, is just what we don't want if we want to access the real truly.

But we have seen that a truth claimed by a knower alludes to dimensions of the self and the world that stretch beyond what the words represent. There's a matchup, but there's a lot of remainder, both in subsidiaries and in prospects. Well-expressed words evoke these hidden dimensions, but they do not drain them of mystery.

We can say that true statements bear on reality, lay hold of a feature of a real. We sense hidden dimensions, which makes us know what we've contacted is real. By definition we couldn't put these into words. Yet we navigate by them in pursuit of the real. We don't have to have articulated future outcomes to grope forward in light of them.

What is more, reality's richness and the way we access it mean that we have in our integration only laid hold of an aspect of the real. We may have a sense of possibilities that don't correspond in a linear way to the nature of the thing. We can get part of it right. In years to come, we may find that we were definitely on to something but had yet to unlock the heart of it. Columbus did not think he had discovered America, for example, even though he knew he was on to something big.

Recently I watched two little boys running in and out of the automatic doors at the public library. Boy #1 knew that his body's presence triggered the door to open. He mistakenly thought the source of this miracle was a protrusion on the left side of the door at his eye level. He would stand in front of it, and nothing would happen. But then littler Boy #2 would run up behind him toward the center of the door, in line with the scanner above the door, and the door would open to admit them both. Boy #1 persisted in his mistake for as long as I waited curbside for my daughter to finish dropping off her books. He knew he was on to something, and experienced some of the possibilities, even though he was noticeably mistaken about the main mechanism. We can have hold of only a piece of the real. Because we have grasped an aspect of reality, we can experience the indicators of the real we have talked about—profoundness of pattern and future prospects—even if we have yet to get the thing entirely right. Thus, the sense of possibilities, like the swinging library door, doesn't guarantee you that your stated thesis is wholly true. It guarantees you that you have got hold of an aspect of reality. Only time tells which aspect you had laid hold of. It may turn out that you were way off; it may turn out that you were more right than you realized.

Obviously what we have seen about knowing calls for more subtlety and humility in our understanding of truth. But far from it undermining the possibility of our contacting the real in our knowing, it confirms it. If we represented the real exhaustively in our articulation, we would conclude that there wasn't much of reality's richness about our statement. It's the evocative and the allusive, as much as the explicit, that links our words to the real. True statements bear indeterminately on reality. But they do bear on reality. What you don't get from their explicit articulation of the real, you get from their evoking it.

None of this implies that we are to give up the effort to articulate and justify our truth claims. Careful thinking and reasoning, while not identical to or exhaustive of truth or knowledge, nevertheless strategically prompts and expands it. That's why going to school and writing papers is still a key to learning. We will always be better for the exercise, and better at skillfully contacting the real. And we will be better at it especially if we do this while understanding that justified belief isn't all there is to knowing, while maintaining a reverence for the indeterminate roots and aspirations of all our epistemic efforts.

All of this calls for us to revise our terminology to match our experience. Instead of *correspondence*, let us speak of *contact*. We lay hold of an aspect of the real.

I think we also need to replace the term *certainty*. When we speak of epistemic success, truth claims that engage the real, the notion of an exhaustive certainty or justification is not only impossible, it is unwanted. It doesn't do justice to the rich fabric of human experience, rooted as it is in our bodies and connecting us to a three-dimensional world, and all of it a motion through time oriented toward the future.

I suggest that a better term is *confidence*. And when I say confidence, I picture St. Louis Cardinals outfielder J. D. Drew hurtling horizontally over the turf to intercept a line drive. Confidence accredits the effort to know in light not only of the reasons we are able to articulate but also of the multitudinous features that we can't put into words, from our felt body sense to our sense of future horizons.

It's been puzzling to think about what it means for a statement to be true, not only because we thought we needed to get outside of ourselves to confirm its correspondence to the real. But we've also been blind to the fact that it takes getting "into" the statement to assess its truth. As we said before, a truth claim is, trivially, a truth claimed. Somehow we thought that the unlived statement was meaningful and testable as true outside of a lived embodiment. But if our statements, like hammers and golf clubs, become explored and known as we embody and use them, then it is only as we get into them and use them that we can say, "This is a good statement," that it does the job well of unlocking the real.

Bottom line, assessing the truth of a claim takes personally getting inside the statement to live it, and it takes embracing the personal responsibility needed to assess the value of the claim. For truth is always personally, responsibly assessed and held. With so many features of our act of knowing that are felt or sensed beyond our articulation, it can only be that assessing truth relies in significant measure on personal appraisal.

Many people believe that the fact that people draw divergent conclusions about the real implies either that there is no objective real or that we must all privatize our claims about truth ("This is true for me, that is true for you."), especially if we are to demonstrate tolerance of all people. Remember the old story of the blind men and the elephant: One man feels the animal's leg and concludes that an elephant is like a tree. Another feels his tail and surmises that an elephant is like a snake. And so on. The moral of the story, however, is precisely the opposite of "There is no objective truth" or "Truth is what I say it is." The moral is that reality is so rich that we had better talk together if we are to stand a chance of figuring it out. Plus, each of us, situated as we are at different vantage points with respect to the real, can contribute unique insights. But we should expect that working together will give us a fuller picture. And that's where articulating and justifying our beliefs together comes into play, relying judiciously on authoritative guides, expanding our horizons, and increasing our grasp on the real.

We contact reality in our acts of knowing—we grasp an aspect of reality. Truth lies in the more-than-verbalizable contact. To this fresh understanding of truth we should respond both with hope and with humility. Humility, because there can never be a procedure by which we can guarantee with certainty or explicitly articulate truth; hope, because for just this reason we confidently access the real in knowing.

▇ Knowing Auto Mechanics and God: The Unfolding Relationship

That it's contact rather than correspondence and confidence rather than certainty is confirmed most readily when it comes to knowing other persons. Were

I to describe someone I knew well to you, my words could well be both apt and allusive. Verbal descriptions are like hoops through which you can jump: they get you moving in the right direction. Jeff is a reliable young mechanic with enough character both to put gas in his mother's tank and to keep a garage of mechanics serving a variety of people over a period of time. But this statement bears a resemblance to the original much as a map resembles a certain countryside. You just have to go for yourself to the Kirkwood Citgo to flesh out the words.

Human persons, what is more, keep unfolding through the years. Once Jeff fixed cars in his parents' garage. Now he and others do it in the bays of his gas station. And third, person-person relationships unfold, too, as each person's response to the other shapes the other.

There came a time some months ago when I told Jeff about this book that I was writing. Typically I never see Jeff. But one cold day I had to take my Taurus over to the station myself and wait while something small was being fixed. I saw him, and I seized the moment: "Jeff, can I talk to you a minute?" "Sure," he said, and led me back to an appropriately grimy office. He greeted my crazy story with a simple smile and "I'll look forward to reading it!" I sent him a copy electronically.

The last time I called and spoke to Bob, the mechanic who usually answers the phone, he answered with his usual, "Hello, Mrs. Meek." But then I heard Jeff's voice in the background. "Is that the famous author?" it thundered. "Tell her I'll change her taillight!" I took my car in later that day. Jeff actually appeared and talked to me for some time while I waited. It was truly a first.

Something inside me protested lightly: you can't talk to me! This isn't the way it happens in the book! My knowing Jeff is interactive. He responds to me, and I to him, and our relationship unfolds, storylike, over time.

The Bible chronicles what theologians call the grand drama of redemption. It is the story of the unfolding relationship, or covenant, between God and his people. God acts, his people respond; his people act, God responds. His unchanging character comes to expression within this relationship in surprising but recognizable ways. While Jesus is God's "final word," in Jesus future surprises are still very much in store for us.

For both auto mechanics and God, as well as with respect to the living world in which we are at home, our words must do more than represent. They must also allude to possibilities, as well as being expected to evoke them.

Also, if we are to appraise the truth of the Bible's words about God, just as with my words about Jeff, we have to live them. Jesus understood this. "If anyone chooses to do God's will, he will find out whether my teaching comes from

139

God or whether I speak on my own." Our Western heritage has, generally speaking, had it backwards: obedience does not require truth; truth requires obedience. Obedience, I like to say, is *lived* truth. Do you want to know my auto mechanic? Live my words. Do you want to know God? Live his words.

For just this same reason if no other, *confidence* better describes the quality of such interpersonal knowing. *Certainty*, as I have used the term, requires there to be exhaustively expressed information that is unavailable as such at the time and in the form in which I rely on it. In knowing I navigate by my reliance on clues and possibilities, shaping and being shaped as my relationship with the known unfolds, trusting, risking, struggling, responding, both recognizing and being surprised as my understanding develops over time. A standard of certainty would paralyze and truncate what is a rich and unfolding epistemic act. It is this way because we are in touch with the real.

For Further Thought and Discussion

Express your thoughts about the discussion: Which term more aptly expresses how we ought to think of truth—*correspondence* or *contact?* Do other common terms, such as *coherence* or *effectiveness*, hold greater promise? Give your reason for what you think. What about *certainty* as over against *confidence?*

Apply it to your experience: How does all this affect the way we proceed in determining whether a claim is true?

18

Engaging and Unlocking the World

Graphic Metaphors for the Act of Knowing

In our knowing, we sense that we have contacted the world by our awareness of both the profundity of our pattern and the hints of future possibilities. Now *contact* solves my adolescent problem of the external world, but the picture it leaves us with is still a bit sterile. When I think about what it means, in our acts of knowing, to contact reality, some other more robust verbs suggest themselves to me. We need verbs that immerse us in the wonderful, exasperating, telltale messiness of word-wielding humans knowing the world.

▌ Unlocking

We can describe our knowing as *unlocking* the world. Our coherent pattern corresponds to the real as a key does to a door, not as a photograph does to its subject. In saying this I address the common misperception that, for our conception to be true, it must accurately picture its referent. This idea fits with the traditional model of knowing: for our perceptual knowledge to be solidly founded, our sense data must mirror without remainder their counterparts in the world. And the idea isn't without its appeal. For the concept I have in my head to be true, it ought to match the way things are so long as you don't think that that is all there is to it.

Aside from the obvious impossibility of stepping outside of ourselves to check in an explicit way that our concept matches the world, the theory also sets the knower over against the world in an unfortunate and ultimately irresolvable way. The model creates "the problem of the external world." Plus, as we've already seen, the model hides the tacit dimensions of our actual experience from us. It hides the human skills in which knowing is rooted and thrives, and it hides the resonances of reality by which we confidently navigate in our knowing.

But now let us think of our conceptions corresponding to reality as a key does to a door. The key-door analogy helps us see that our conceptions, if they are apt, gain us access to uncharted regions beyond. In the coherence we glimpse fresh vistas, vistas that include depth, horizons, and hidden possibilities. But even as the key that unlocks a door lets us out, it also lets reality in.

A pattern achieved unlocks the real, much as a key does a door. Before we understood the role of blood, or of germs, or of bacteria, a lot of people and animals died through bloodletting, poor hygiene, and bacterial infections. New coherences unlocked critical doors to reality. People now live through illnesses that once would have killed them. Think of the possibilities unleashed through these discoveries.

The real world gives back, and it gives as good as it gets. How could we ever think that in knowing the knower determines reality? Try telling that to a tidal wave, or to your motion-sick stomach. Reality too often knocks us over. It might as well be saying: You treat me right and maybe, if you're lucky, I might treat you right! There are centers of meaning and activity there. They respond to us. Our integrative patterns evoke the real.

◼ Engaging

Our integrative patterns also *engage* the real. They engage us in the real. You learn to sink the basketball in the hoop 85 percent of the time. You have successfully engaged the world. Professional baseball players are such reliable fielders that they actually are charged with errors on the rare occasions when they miss. That's engaging the world. When you understand the theory of relativity (they tell me) it opens wide vistas on the world to which you were previously blind. Your successful "making sense of experience" roots you more solidly and more profoundly in reality.

Some funny flowers are currently blooming in my garden. I first encountered them in my neighbor's garden when our family moved to St. Louis eleven years ago. One day in late July, the flowers were suddenly there, where they had not been before. Next spring I learned that the bulbs put up very bulb-like leaves at the same time that daffodils come up and bloom. But there are no flowers. The leaves gradually die back and have disappeared by midsummer. They are called surprise lilies.

One morning you visit the garden, long after you have forgotten the disappointment of the flowerless leaves. And you are surprised. Now you have leafless stalks crowned with pale pink trumpets. There is no doubt they are lilies: the blooms are little pink versions of other lilies you know.

The name that you now speak knowingly gives you the aptest of handles on the whole experience. You'll never forget what they're called, what they do, and what they look like. The words engage the world. They root you in the real.

Oh—in the South, I'm told, they have an additional name. They're called naked ladies. There's something to that label, too! It captures the pinkness, the bareness, and the element of surprise!

When we think of our numerous day-to-day experiences of it, it would hardly occur to us that our knowing prevented or called into question our access to something beyond us, or that our pattern making negated what is in fact a palpable submission to it. Our integrative pattern roots us in the world even as it is rooted in us. The patterns are handles, tools, keys. If they're good, they extend us and develop our world. They actually expand the possibilities.

Why, after all, is human knowing full of essential, inarticulable, and indeterminate features? Knowing is this way precisely because it is embedded at both anchor points in the real. How can it be this way if human knowing is not rooted in the thickness of a world, a world engaged by embodied agents of knowing? If knowing were as on the traditional model, a sentence made sterile by an exhaustive lucidity, there could be no room for bodies and world. It would be the mindless workings of a robot. It is just the messiness of it that tells us that we engage the real. Again I speak misleadingly, when I say "messiness": only from the point of view of an impossible and sterile ideal of fully articulable and justifiable knowledge is it messy. From within our everyday experience it is the lived and sensed rootedness of our acts of knowing.

▮ Knowing Auto Mechanics and God: Unlocking and Engaging the World

Knowing Jeff to be a reliable auto mechanic gives me a wonderful handle on my world. In it I unlock and engage reality. I can relax about my auto service needs. I can confidently drive an ancient car around the city knowing that he is a phone call away. I don't waste emotional energy fretting about whether he has actually fixed what he said he fixed, or whether he has fixed the right thing. The dipping checking account is sobering, but I believe making payments would be worse. And I believe it a reasonable trade-off for reliable service. In fact, I live more than I speak my beliefs about Jeff: I just use him with confidence, entrusting my car needs to him and getting on with the rest of my life. You should be so fortunate!

Similarly, knowing God has unlocked the world for me. In knowing him I engage the world. To affirm "I believe in God, the Father Almighty, Maker of heaven and earth; and in Jesus Christ, his only Son, our Lord . . ." opens vista upon vista. You can see a tree as a chance collocation of atoms, randomly evolved from a primordial soup. You can see a tree as conforming to impersonal laws that regulate its behavior. But these come up short: neither tells us why the tree is there, why it is reliably there, and why I should respectfully get to know it. But see the tree as a thing made and moved by the utterly faithful words of an infinite person for his own delight, one whose ways we will know better as we as we explore the tree, and you have unlocked both the wonder of the tree and the majesty of God. Plus, you grasp yourself better, too: you are a knower who images and walks before God among the other things he has made. You are not God. They are not God. But you and they are made by him and thus fraught with significance and value. And you are the one of the two of you given the job of caring for the other. The tree needs you to image God in calling forth its glory (water and fertilizer and pruning, thank you very much, resulting in fruit and cures for cancer) and in combating its brokenness and yours (stamping out carpenter ants and fungus, designating national forests, authorizing protective underbrush burning). In knowing God, I engage and unlock the world.

As you read through this book, you may be feeling that the Christianity I describe does not fit with your previous impression of it. I'm hoping that what you perceive in these pages is the richness and vibrancy of Christianity, along with the richness of the world. One reason for the discrepancy between what you might have thought and what you read here is, I believe, epistemological, related directly to this book's topic. The modern model of human knowing, I am arguing, was a truncated version, promoting a sterile disconnectedness from the real, and from ourselves and others. The ideal of knowledge as statements and proof leads us to discredit and overlook more-than-articulable dimensions of our knowing. I believe that the Christian church in recent centuries has absorbed this model. I find many Christians who are concerned to see the Bible as offering a set of propositions about God, and who believe that all their claims must be thoroughly proven, justified, to be credible to themselves and to others. Christianity has been marked by modernism. And while Christians feel the threat of postmodernism, we have often been blind to our own modernist concessions. Thus, while society at large may have moved on to more of a postmodernist stance, Christianity has remained a harbor of modernism. We have been blind, additionally, to the misfit between our default modernist model of knowledge and the Scripture. We have thus been blinded to the epistemological riches of Scripture.

One of my students opened my eyes to this. "You've given me back my Christianity," he said. "All my life I have looked for hidden compartments and secret doors. I became a Christian as an adult, being drawn by the richness of knowing God. But I soon was led to believe that being a good Christian was all about defending the propositions of your faith rationally. It took the magic out of it. Now you tell me about knowing as unlocking a door, and it restores the magic. Now I have something to say again to my unbelieving brother."

Your fundamental approach to knowledge, whether you've thought about it or not, can make a big difference. And it makes a difference in knowing both auto mechanics and God.

For Further Thought and Discussion

Find personal examples. Can you think of some of your own stories of integrations in which you have unlocked or engaged the world? In these stories name particular ways the world "knocked you over," or the way you "opened up the world" through your fresh focus. When you think about experiences such as these, do you feel that you connect with the world through your efforts?

Consider your experience of reality. Do you agree that, if we as knowers are situated in an inexhaustively rich world, contacting the real ought very well to feel like opening a door to let in more than you expected? Why or why not?

Consider your experience of God. Is your experience of God of the unlocking and engaging sort? In what ways?

19

The Power of the Pattern

Submitting to the Authority of Our Creations, Both Before and After We Meet Them

The act of knowing involves the knower in exercising profound responsibility and choice. Over the course of a discovery or a "learning," we must first entrust ourselves to the tutelage of an authority who teaches us how to see and what to look for. It means submitting to being retaught. We need to exercise the effort to gain the skills that purchase our entrance to the playing field, so to speak. We must rely on those skills as we launch out into the unknown. We must start to reassign significances, guided by an as yet unspecified goal. This involves having confidence in our ability to be guided in this way. It involves challenging previous expectations of the way things ought to be. Along the way we take risks as we think things like "There's a problem here," or "There's something here I need to learn," and then "Now that's significant, but I don't yet know why," and "That's a clue," and then "I'm getting closer to figuring it out." It means entrusting ourselves to the particular features of the as yet unachieved integration, struggling to embody them in an effort to access their meaning. It means, after a time, picking out a pattern at a point when so much is hidden that to affirm the existence of a pattern may involve a resolute and risky choice. Finally, the human knower's exercise of profound responsibility involves him in submitting to the authoritative reality of the pattern he chose.

The point of the paragraph is that human knowing is through and through an active exercise of personal responsibility. The point of the chapter is that, nevertheless, human knowing involves submission to the authoritative reality of our personal integrative achievement. Together, these make human knowing a responsible submission to the real.

Centuries of Western philosophy have led to our thinking that for knowledge to be objective and certain, the personal responsibility of the knower must be minimized to the point of elimination. We have glorified an impersonalism and called it objectivity. And while it is right to avoid subjectivism, conclusions skewed away from accuracy by a warped outlook, we have attempted to throw the proverbial baby out with the bathwater. We have held up an ideal of knowing that is unworkable and untrue to the human experience. In doing this we have been guilty of irresponsibility in our knowing. We've tried to let ourselves off the hook.

More recently, we have recognized that human involvement cannot be eliminated from our truth claims. It's led us to the other extreme: we've thrown a different baby out with the bathwater. This time the baby is truth and reality: no truth, no reality, except the truth and reality I make. If the former error was letting ourselves off the hook, maybe this is making ourselves into the hook. What we fail to see is that this is equally irresponsible. We no longer have to submit to an independent reality or truth.

Sometimes the value of the approach is defended in the name of tolerance of other persons' truths and realities. Our society feels that this is its supreme value. We fail to recognize the profound intolerance that lurks in the view, not to mention disrespect of others' commitments. We also fail to see that nobody would want to practice this approach consistently, even if they could.

You hear the screams of your neighbor, a young single woman. Some sort of bodily attack is in progress. Do you respect the reality and truth of the intruder by tolerating his behavior? Would you not in the process be disrespecting the reality and truth of your neighbor?

The human experience regularly requires and appraises the risk of commitment to truth, to the rightness and wrongness of action. I intervened in my daughters' lives, for example, to insist on piano lessons as long as we were able to afford it. I refused to entertain complaints. A year or so ago I heard my youngest, now almost fourteen, tell someone that my policy "had worked," meaning that they all like music and recognize that they are skilled now in a way they would not have been had I not violated their personal space. I silently

147

exulted, realizing that my responsible risk had paid off, but realizing, humbly, that it might not have. Such decisions are regular occurrences in parenting. The emergency room offers another hotbed of such examples.

It is not responsible to deny objective truth and reality in knowing; it is irresponsible. It is not responsible to make the human knower or community of knowers the arbiters of a private truth and reality; it is irresponsible.

It is not possible to avoid personal and communal responsibility in knowing. What we need to see is that personal and communal responsibility in knowing is the sole vehicle for profoundly accessing the objectively real.

▌ Submitting to the Reality of Our Patterns

The coherent pattern we achieve, confirmed as it is by how it transforms our particulars and ourselves and how it evokes reality, comes to exercise a kind of authority over us. It tends to take on a life of its own, to start calling the shots. We may have exercised tremendous responsibility and risk to access it. But part of this responsible behavior is to allow it to shape us. It is a submission to our own achievement as real, true, and even authoritative.

In the movie classic *White Christmas*, former World War II infantrymen, now entertainers, Bob and Phil (Bing Crosby and Danny Kaye) encounter their former beloved and feared general, now an innkeeper fallen on hard times. In the moment when Danny Kaye first sees the general, he sees a janitor. Then he recognizes his face. He drops his suitcases and straightens to an alarmed salute. The real, once we have accessed it, often has that effect. A salute is a submission to reality.

Authors and sculptors testify to their submission to the internal coherence of their own creation by saying that it came to shape their work, rather than the other way around. Frankenstein's monster is a graphic version of this!

My Fair Lady was inspired by the story of Pygmalion: a sculptor plies his craft so superbly that the resultant statue becomes real. Henry Higgins makes Eliza Doolittle his linguistic project: in teaching her to speak properly he fools all the snobbish ears of English society concerning her background. But then he falls in love with the woman he has made, submitting to the powerful reality of his own creation.

The coherence resulting from an epistemic act becomes a standard by which we interpret ourselves and our world. It has reshaped our sense of what is rational. It has reshaped us. Now it operates normatively, and we judge ourselves and our experiences in its light.

Once a baby has identified a ball, for example, all spherical objects, yea, all remotely spherical objects, might be judged in light of the standard and used in throwing!

Consider crystals. People dig crystals out of the ground and evaluate them, not in reference to all the other crystals that have been unearthed, but in reference to a geometrically perfect ideal that exists only as a concept.

The St. Louis Science Center contains a skewed room. Inside the room you see that the floor and ceiling and walls intersect at something drastically other than right angles. You are instructed to stand a child in one corner and an adult in the other, then to go outside the room and peer into it through a crack. The crack serves to eliminate all peripheral clues. What you see when you look through the crack is a perfectly square room, with a very tiny adult in one corner and a very large child in the other! Your eyes expect rooms to be square, so much so that they compensate by readjusting the relative heights of the people in it!

There's a kind of backwardness to our integrative pattern making. We've said before that it's not as if you could begin with the particulars relevant to the pattern and then reason your way to the pattern, as from premises to a conclusion. In a profound and curious way, the pattern *comes first*. It does not come first in time. But it comes first in priority, and then the moment of integrative success has a kind of retroactive power. It's always in light of our postintegration hindsight that we see the clues, finally, for what they are. At the time we were relying on them, we could not have explicitily ascribed to them the very meaning we surmised that they had. But in working retroactively, the pattern serves normatively, after the fact, giving the clues their status and meaning as clues. We allow it to interpret our experience. We submit to its reality.

Actually, there is a sense in which the pattern often does come first in time, as well as in priority. In the Foreword, I dedicated this book to my philosophy teacher and mentor, Jim Grier. I spoke of being drawn, on first hearing of him, by the possibility of indeterminate future manifestations. Literally, that is what happened. I had a conversation with a student of his whom I met. As that young man excitedly described what he was learning in his classes from this great man, my heart was burning within me. I felt as if my eyes had been opened to what I really wanted to pursue. In twelve hours I had made the decision to change colleges and majors to study with this man, a decision that has radically shaped the unfolding of my life and vocation. I could not have even specified the pattern, yet it was already influencing me, drawing me. I think all of us go through experiences like this as we do what we call "pursuing our calling"—or, as one young artist friend recently put it, "finding my voice."

149

Counselors make the case that what you envision shapes you. We get what we expect to get. Their point is that, therefore, we can shape ourselves by shaping what we envision. The Bible, by the way, confirms this: "He who seeks good finds good will, but evil comes to him who searches for it." I find that this profound and somewhat unnerving insight exemplifies the power of the pattern.

Because of the normativity it exercises, the pattern we have achieved in our integrative effort resists our discrediting it. C. S. Lewis talks of the obstinacy of belief. This is true whether the belief in question is in a ball, a mechanic, or God. We are disinclined to entertain counterproposals, for the pattern has so transformed the clues (our body sense included) that we are ill equipped to recognize counterevidence.

■ Knowing Auto Mechanics and God: The Authoritative Power of the Pattern

You can tell, I'm sure, that I like my auto mechanic, Jeff. You can tell by my commitment to him. In fact, you've probably seen that my conception of him as a reliable auto mechanic actually shapes how I interpret new information that comes my way. I am disposed to interpret information in his favor, even information originating from my own sense perception! It's not that I can't conceive of any sort of information that would lead me to find another mechanic. But it is the case that I resist interpretations that would lead to this. My concept of Jeff shapes my expectation also about what makes a good auto mechanic. I am liable to employ it as I assess your relationship to your mechanic, for example, which may not be as favorable.

A person's concept of God involves the same sort of obstinate normativity. To know the God of the Bible is to know a being who claims supreme authority over all of life. Actually, those who reject the concept of God do so, I believe, for fear of the very same thing. For to know God is to submit to him. All those who have struggled to understand who he is by piecing together the pattern of their lives and of this world in light of Scripture's guidance come to acknowledge the existence of a divine person who seriously outranks them.

C. S. Lewis takes issue with anyone who tries to hold that Jesus was a great moral teacher. That is one interpretation of the Gospels' accounts of Jesus' life that simply will not do. Whatever Jesus was, he simply could not have been merely a great moral teacher. For Jesus repeatedly claimed to be God. We are left with three possibilities: either he is a liar, or he is a lunatic ("along the lines of the man who claims he is a poached egg"), or he is who he claims to be—

150

supreme Lord. If either of the first two alternatives is correct, you would definitely not consider Jesus a great moral teacher. You would not want your children to be near him. Only the third alternative is both consistent with the claims Jesus made and a favorable interpretation of his character. But then, only one bodily posture, so to speak, remains to us: falling to our knees before him.

A person's belief in God also, appropriately, exercises a normativity over his or her life and experience. I tend to resist interpretations of events that discredit his claims. When faced with a puzzling situation, I give him the benefit of the doubt; I hold out for a possible alternative explanation that is consistent with his claims.

This obstinacy of belief is not immune to every conceivable counterattack. The most commonly perceived threat to belief in God is what we call the problem of evil. The presence of pain and suffering in this world and within our own experience challenges our integrative hold on God. And, of course, the real problem of pain is not the abstract, "armchair" one. It is the agony of the one in its throes, the one whose brain frequencies are jammed by pain, prevented from lofty thoughts through bodily affliction. In some extreme situations no sentences or words seem to pertain at the time.

Yet I would say to you that however you resolve the problem of evil, there is one kind of alternative that simply will not do. It is to say that evil is not a problem, that evil is the way it is supposed to be, or that it is no different in value from events deemed good. This simply does not accord with our experience. One cannot be raped and call it good. One cannot call injustice or oppression good. Whoever you are, there is something in your life or your experiences that you think is or was really, outrageously wrong. I felt this, I remember, when I looked into my father-in-law's coffin at a beautifully suited, beloved, dead man. I felt outrage. This was not the way it was supposed to be.

But if evil challenges my belief in the existence of God, my sense of outrage at things not the way they are supposed to be challenges a belief in his nonexistence. A universe without a standard of good would be one in which you and I would feel no such outrage at evil. If belief in God has a problem with evil, nonbelief in God has a greater problem with evil. Additionally, nonbelief in God, I believe, has a corresponding problem of good: how to do justice to human ideals and loves, to objective beauty and goodness in the world. Belief in God has no such corresponding problem.

But this kind of wrestling with possible gaps and challenges to our integrative acts of knowing God does not discredit them as epistemic acts. Rather, it confirms that it is in this respect just like all other human acts of knowing. Far, far more is at stake in the decision. The issue of God being who the Bible claims him to be affects every area of our lives and of the world. But then, that's what you would expect of knowing a being who is Lord of the universe.

My belief in God is obstinate. It exercises authority over all of my life. I interpret—in fact I try to interpret—every experience in light of his Word, the Bible. But in being obstinate, my belief is thereby neither irrational nor a perversion of objectivity. In its obstinacy it matches every other act of human knowing. In its obstinacy it is profoundly human. With respect to the normativity of our integrative achievement of knowing, knowing God bears a remarkable similarity to knowing my auto mechanic.

All of us, I believe, feel that we are searching, longing for something. I described this longing in an earlier chapter as a longing for transcendence, or for glory. Could it be that our longing is the draw of a pattern whose power operates even in advance of our discovery of it? I would like humbly to suggest that what we are all longing for is God. In Augustine's familiar words: "Thou hast made us for Thyself, and our hearts are restless until they find their rest in Thee."

For Further Thought and Discussion

Name your powerful patterns. Which of your beliefs are obstinate, exercising power over large areas of your life? In what ways do they act as norms rather than conclusions or descriptions? Are you satisfied with your prevailing patterns? In what ways do they fall short? Can such obstinate beliefs be revised?

Describe your personal experience. Have you had experiences in which a pattern was drawing you, even though you weren't sure what it was? Is this a good way to describe what it means to long to know something? What do you think you are ultimately longing for? What is your response to the idea that your ultimate longing might be for God?

PART V

Loving the Longing

20

Getting It Wrong

Mistaken Acts of Knowing

Here is a chapter whose time has come! I can well imagine that you have been reading chapter after chapter and saying, "Yes, BUT . . ."! "Yes, I see all the features of the act of knowing that you describe; yes, I can think of applications of the model in my own life; yes, I see the parallels that you are drawing. BUT . . . is it possible to be mistaken? If all human knowing is integration, and some people believe *A*, and some people believe *Not A*, how can these both be acts of *knowing*? And, at bottom, perhaps, how can I be certain I'm not wrong—about my auto mechanic or about God? How can you, Esther Meek, be certain that you are not wrong about knowing?" It's time we talk about these things.

▉ How Mistaken Integrations Happen

First, as I'm sure you can see, mistaken claims are not unique to the model of knowing we've been talking about. No matter what you think about knowing and knowledge, mistaken conclusions occur, and they cause consternation. On the old model of knowledge, false claims are handled neatly by saying that they are not knowledge. This tactic is reflected in the way we use the word *know.* You can't say you know something once you find out that it is false. But this is

155

a little like the childish game participant who rewrites the rules as she goes so that she always wins. It begs the question of *how* we are to know what is knowledge and what isn't.

The reality of mistakes is a main reason why I choose to speak not of knowledge but of acts of knowing, or epistemic acts. I believe it is appropriate to describe some acts as acts of knowing, epistemic efforts, even when they are partly mistaken. "Act of knowing" can refer to the attempt without implying its utter success. Moreover, integrations can be just plain mistaken.

There are three basic features of our day-to-day experience that lead me to hold out for this. One is that when we observe someone integrating to what we know to be a mistaken pattern, we still observe the features of an integrative act: we see them actively shaping hitherto unrelated particulars into a coherent whole. Another is that partially mistaken discoveries and claims nevertheless in some measure can and do access reality.

A third is that, given the nature of human knowing as described here, it is appropriate and also unavoidable for knowers to affirm with confidence truth claims that might be turn out to be false. That confident risk is both less and more than a sterile certainty. The mix of clues and prospects on which we rely contains no "givens," for no piece of our experience is what it is apart from our assigning it its significance; and about no piece of our experience are we above being in error. But in this discussion I hope we have come to appreciate, and feel within ourselves, the aptness, humility, and joy of skilled, epistemic risk reaching for the world.

Of course, from the knower's point of view, a coherent pattern probably contains nothing in it that he or she would explicitly identify as "mistakes." Instead, he or she may simply be caught up in the pattern's glory. Or, the knower may move past the mistaken areas as hiddennesses, to which he or she extends the overall interpretation flowing from the pattern. Or, the knower may identify these areas as puzzles or anomalies, clues that point to yet further possibilities.

Did Christopher Columbus make a great discovery? Yes. Did he discover what he thought he had discovered? No. To his mind he had not discovered America. He thought he had gotten to the East by going west, treating literally the assumption that the world was round.

Did Joseph Priestley discover oxygen? We credit him for the discovery. But he thought what he had discovered was dephlogistated air. The candle in the sealed space went out when the air was full of phlogiston, not, he thought, because it was depleted of oxygen.

Did Copernicus get it right about the planets revolving around the sun? Yes. Would he have been surprised that their orbits were elliptical rather than circular? As a good classical thinker, he would have abhorred the thought of this impurity in perfect motion. It took a century of worldview change to accommodate this insight of Kepler's.

We are right to consider each of these efforts *discoveries*. Each of them at the time held the promise of unspecifiable future possibilities. Each was felt by its author to orchestrate profoundly and unspecifiably the features of their experience. Each discovery thereby indicated that its author had made contact with the real. None was mistake-free.

Acts of knowing are not restricted to the science lab. Just about every human act is an act of knowing. To live is to know, where knowing is humans engaging the world, actively and responsibly submitting to reality.

Our simplest seeing is interpretive and integrative. Seeing is powerfully persuasive, but seeing itself is always shaped, for good or ill, by our conceptions and commitments. It is not the case simplistically that seeing is believing. Even in our simplest seeing we can be mistaken.

In Shakespeare's *Much Ado About Nothing*, Claudio sees his fiancée, Hero, amorously involved with another man on the eve of the wedding. (I have in mind the scenes from Kenneth Branagh's film version.) This is what he believes he sees. We know he sees another woman being called "Hero" in the act. He is guided in his seeing by the evilly intentioned brother of his friend, the count. He chooses not to believe Hero's professions of unalloyed love, nor the testimonials of his gracious and good host, Hero's father. Claudio concludes that Hero is "not a maid," and he publicly defames her. The play is aptly named. Shakespeare is describing a mistaken integration.

Psychiatrist David Burns, in his book *Feeling Good: The New Mood Therapy*, describes a series of "cognitive distortions," to which human beings are prone. They include: all-or-nothing thinking, overgeneralization, jumping to conclusions, labeling, personalization, and so on. He documents common chains of reasoning about circumstances that involve these distortions. "I didn't get an A-plus on this project, so I am worthless" is an example of all-or-nothing thinking. His thesis is that people can change the way they feel by changing the way they think about circumstances. He teaches his readers to counteract cognitive distortions by identifying them and replacing them with more realistic patterns, or by refraining from unwarranted pattern making.

Are not these cognitive distortions so many propensities to mistaken integration? We can be inclined to believe the worst about ourselves or about others. And, more basically, we are inclined simply to make sense of our experience, compelled to integrate the circumstances of our lives into some meaningful

157

pattern. The patterns aren't always well founded. And even if they are well founded, the integrations still can be in some measure mistaken.

Let's look a little more closely at the features of the integrative act, so as to understand how mistakes happen. Whenever we integrate to a coherent pattern, relying on an array of clues and guided by hints of possibilities, connecting the dots in a way that interprets both the visible and the invisible, we can get it partly wrong.

On the one hand, I surmise that it is unlikely, unless there are unusual circumstances, that an integration would be wholly wrong. On the other hand, it is unlikely that any integration is wholly right. Why would an integration rarely be wholly wrong? It is because we are embodied knowers rooted in a world of embodied characters. Significant portions of the clues we rely on lie beyond our ability to control. Clues deep within our bodies and characteristic features of the world around us fall in this category. In computerese, we might call this hardwiring. One cannot be mistaken about the harmful properties of fire or poison and continue to live and know! With regard to key features of human experience, to be mistaken is to be dead. To continue to live is to get at least some things right.

Why would an integration rarely be wholly right? There are a number of reasons. It is because the world we seek to understand is inexhaustibly rich. It is because the knower's engaging of the world is itself a profoundly complex act, embedded as it is in a real knower and a real known. It is because the human, the world, and the knowing all move and develop through time. All these factors mean that any time-bound statement grasps only the hem of the robe of reality. Our words can be simultaneously poorer and richer than we realize. Take, for example, what a female student recently told me: "My husband, John, cares for me so much!" She proceeded to tell me how, while she had been away, he had built special drawers and shelves into their pantry. I imagine that, even before they were married two years ago, she would have said, "John cares for me so much!" At that time, she probably had no thought of pantry shelves in mind. At that time, he probably didn't either. Her statement before the marriage said both more and less than she knew.

Because integration is a transforming act rather than a sterile step-by-step procedure, it is somewhat forgiving of error. Integration involves the knower responsibly (though not necessarily consciously) assigning varied significances to the clues before and within him or her. The resulting coherence is more like a vision than a deduction. It incorporates a measure of risk, and always a measure of conjecture.

The integrative effort is successful to the degree that it lays hold of an aspect of reality. A truth claim may grasp reality more or less profoundly. It is a matter of degree; the possible percentages are not limited to 0 or 100. A truth claim may grasp reality profoundly even if a good portion of it is mistaken. Remember Columbus.

In our knowing we can experience a sense of future possibilities, even when our integrative achievement is partly mistaken, when the achievement has nevertheless engaged reality in some measure. Discoverers get excited when they know they are on to something, even when they are not able to tell you exactly what that something is. And that's in some measure legitimate. It has to be, or we could never move from unknowing to knowing. But we do move from unknowing to knowing.

Our integrative efforts unlock doors. Fresh conceptions are so many keys that open fresh vistas on the real. They bind us ever more firmly in it. But conceptions gone bad are keys that lock doors, obscure vistas, and disconnect us from the world. Perhaps we have held the conception too rigidly. Perhaps we have ceased the ongoing intuitive measurement and modification of it by which we navigate the world. Perhaps we settled for a pattern that falls short of something more apt. Perhaps we have by a chain of faulty integrations become blind to whole domains of our lives. Perhaps we have rejected the life-giving word of an authoritative guide.

■ Hope for the Mistaken

But where you can be wrong, you can also be right. "Mistakes" are only meaningful as such if there is a right or a true or a real to be attained. If there is no truth, there can be no mistakes. But we make mistakes. We know this from everyday experience. We know we make mistakes. We know what it is to correct our mistakes. So there must be truth, a getting it right about the way things are, truth to which we aspire, truth that we long for, a longing that makes us the humans we are.

Remember the film *A Beautiful Mind*. We can get it wrong. We can also get it right. A beautiful mind is one that pursues right integrations, truth and reality, even when it is hard and costly. Why should we prefer the real and the true? No justification is ever offered. But as humans, we don't need one.

How can we be certain that we are making a mistake or that we are getting it right? By now you ought to recognize a pitfall lurking in the word *certain!* Truth lies in its indeterminate bearing on reality. Certainty is not to be had, nor would we want the detached sterility it requires. But we are not left with subjectivism, relativism, and skepticism. We are set free to love the risk and the responsibility that draws us deeper into the world.

You may be wondering if the many unverbalizable components of knowing are the culprits, the source of errors in our truth claims. I suppose I could say yes to this, although I'm not completely sure this is an accurate way to say it. But we have to remember that we have acknowledged the indeterminacies in our knowing, not because we thought they do or don't introduce errors, but because they are there. They are there because as knowers we are embodied humans embedded in a world. Writing the indeterminacies back out of our model of knowing won't make them go away. Nor would it make the errors go away. We were not better at truth on the old model of knowledge. We were successful in knowing on the old model, actually, in spite of the fact that the old model blinded us to integral features of our knowing. We should be that much better at our knowing for accrediting them.

It is helpful to remember that knowing is a skill. Our skill at accessing reality is partly a matter of latent talent. Some people have been blessed with a superior aptitude for engaging the real. Others, we might say, seem out of touch. But our skill at accessing reality in our knowing is also partly a matter of practice. The more we do it, the better and faster we become. In this, knowing is no different from shooting basketballs. Even the best player we know does not make every shot. But we pay big money to hire the ones with high percentages.

The fact that our knowing can be improved with practice suggests what we are to do about mistakes! You may have been thinking, Are we just condemned to be mistaken? Never to recognize and avoid mistakes? If so, does this not radically undermine the whole endeavor of human knowing? No, no, and yes, it would.

Just consider once again the analogy of knowing to any other skill, say, competitive speed skating. People who go far in the competitions, to the Olympics, for example, are people who have practiced, people who rigorously scrutinize their own physical efforts, their "inner game," and even the clothes they wear, with an eye to being better at what they do.

The skill of knowing is no different. Let's talk about developing an effective relationship with a friend or family member. That involves coming to know that person over time. Effective relationships are built on truthful knowing, not on persistent and careless mistakes. Cognitive distortions, of the sort I described earlier, do not enhance relationships. They deserve to be challenged.

It's important to see that thinking of knowing as an active shaping of particulars into a coherent whole that indicates contact with reality, an act that relies on ranges of indeterminacy, an act that is open to error—thinking of knowing in this way does not let us off the hook when it comes to responsibility. In fact, it summons us to greater responsibility. The whole point is that we can and must do something to increase our skill, to avoid mistakes. The encouragement that motivates us is that the possibility of mistakes does not undermine the possibility of knowing, or the longing to know. We can and do know. We long to do it better.

In this lies the tremendous value of the traditional model of knowing that I have so consistently criticized. What I have criticized about it is that it misleads us about key dimensions essential to knowing. Also, it ultimately snuffs out hope as to the possibility of our success, not only with respect to knowing God, but with respect to knowing anything at all. We need to restore the hope and the insight of ordinary human experience. But traditional philosophy and epistemology teach us a rigor in our scrutiny of our claims and how we justify them that we would do well to keep. We need to keep this rigor and discipline because knowing is a skill that can be improved through remedial effort.

▪ Coping with Mistakes

How do we ever find out that we have made a mistake? In our ordinary experience, we can identify a couple of regularly used methods. One is time, and the other one, closely related, is perspective.

Some mistakes simply can't stand unchallenged for long. And it is reality that, in time, challenges them. As knowers we are embodied and rooted in a world. Our rootedness works to keep us honest. One could not be mistaken concerning the safety of drinking poison for long. Also over time we are able to gauge more fully the ways in which certain claims were right and the ways in which they were mistaken. Think of Copernicus's claim, for example. Kepler helped us eventually to see that it was right to say that the sun was the center of the planetary system, but that it was wrong to represent the planets' orbits as purely circular.

Mistakes, in the long run, either get corrected or do great damage—and then get corrected. However fallible our efforts, we are rooted in a world that has an objective character; we abuse it to our peril and bless it to our own blessing. We used to think that any fire at all was bad for forests; we have come to see that controlled fire helps keep trees strong and retards undergrowth, and that even uncontrolled fire acts as a positive catalyst for some things in a forest habitat, such as the germination of some kinds of seeds. It took a few decades of

161

Smokey the Bear's calling our attention to fire to make us think better of and revise our claims. So time works to help us see our mistakes.

My husband and I remember seeing a public television documentary on the infrastructure of New York City. We remember in particular the wry comment of an official in waste management. "I have no doubt we will eventually clean up the environment," he said. "Sooner or later, *the trash will win.*" (This statement has come to be a useful maxim in our household.) Mistakes, like the trash, have the last word, so to speak, and we can deny them no longer.

Someone else's perspective often helps us see our mistakes, also. The act of knowing, as we have seen, involves relying on clues close to us to focus on something beyond. The very structure, while it engages us with the world, holds the potential for blinding us to some things. We can be especially blind to the things that we rely on that are close to us, whether they are bodily behaviors or philosophical assumptions. It often takes the challenge of someone whose word we trust to help us to revise the underpinnings of our seeing.

Think of Claudio in *Much Ado About Nothing.* Reality breaking in over time, and the challenges of others, helped him recognize his mistake. A comically stupid policeman overhears an accomplice boast of his part in the plot to deceive Claudio. Plus, those who know Hero's character, whose caring truthfulness Claudio also respects, reject his behavior as despicable. Had Hero truly been guilty, her family and friends would have not been so completely confident of her character. Or, if they were perpetrating a deceit, Claudio would not be justified in respecting them and their characters. This must cause profound discomfort and self-doubt for Claudio. As a member of the audience, I say—Good! He deserves it!

C. S. Lewis, in an essay by this title, recommends "the reading of old books." Every age in history is especially blind to its own assumptions. When you read books from a different era, you will be helped to see what your own age overlooks. For while they will exhibit the characteristic blindness of their own age, their blindness falls in different areas from yours. Juxtaposing the one to the other enables us to navigate forward in our understanding. Reading old books is one way we correct our mistakes by relying on others' perspective. Part of growing in skill as knowers involves, as we discussed before, growing our sense of whom to trust as a guide with respect to what.

One of the commonly known facts of life is that we learn from our mistakes. We ruefully laugh about gaining experience. I suggest that this fact of life makes no sense on the modern model of knowledge, or a postmodern one, but does make sense when we think of knowing as active pattern making to make sense of the world.

The integrative model of knowing offers a realistic understanding of mistakes and how we deal with them. It matches our ordinary experience. A model of knowing that stipulates exhaustive lucidity dismisses mistakes as non-knowledge. Skepticism as a model, disallowing as it does the possibility of truth, can't even use the word "mistake."

■ Knowing Auto Mechanics and God: Getting It Wrong and Getting It Right

Could I be mistaken about my auto mechanic's reliability? Of course. If I were wholly mistaken, my car might not run as well as it does. Suppose I am being a bit sanguine about his reliability; then it is fair to say I am partially mistaken in my claim that he is reliable. He is, after all, human. But my car is, after all, still running.

Is there any way that I could be certain of his reliability—a certainty that would be immune to mistakes? No. Do I know all there is to know about Jeff? Do I know all there is to know about him as a mechanic? No. But do any of these things force the conclusion that I do not or cannot know him?

Do any of these things compel me to retreat to pat social niceties such as "You have your truth and I have mine" or "My choice is a personal and private matter" or "—As long as you're happy"? No. The issue is not my personal happiness; it is the well-being of my car. If I think I make my own truth about my auto mechanic, why can I not just make my own truth about my auto, and save the time and expense of an auto mechanic?

The fact that I can be wrong about my mechanic's reliability means that I can move toward being right. I can think carefully about his work, and about what I know of his character. I can revise my claims in light of my ongoing experience. I can assess the strength of my own conclusions. I can invest in thinking systematically about how I know anything at all—which is just what we're doing at the moment!

Could I be mistaken about God? Yes, I could. In healthy measure my claims about God hang on my trust in the words of the Bible's writers, which though recorded over millennia consistently unite to affirm that Jesus is God and that he will return to save and to judge. Could they have been wrong? It's possible. Could I be mistaking their import? Possibly; certainly in some measure. Can I nevertheless see that I am involved in an act of knowing with respect to God—an integrative pattern making to which I submit as it engages me in the world? Profoundly yes. Can I come to understand better, increase my skill at knowing

God? Yes. My knowing will inevitably benefit when I study the Bible and the world carefully, think through my "inner game," trying to embody what my coaches are saying.

Another reason we make mistakes in any area of knowing is that our character is bent. We do not always want what is good. Even when we know what is good, however we may define good, we do not always strive for it. Often our desires do not measure up to the standard we set for ourselves, much less anybody else's standard. And these desires are an unavoidable ingredient in the passionate disposing of ourselves, the personal clues that shape our knowing and acting. Often we see what we want to see. And what we want to see is sometimes bent.

I want to think well of myself, for example. I don't see, or I don't take seriously, the things I do wrong. I do not deal them into my knowing of myself. When it comes to knowing God, things go even more awry. We are bent to worship the wrong things; we resist worshiping the right one. It cannot help but cloud our knowing, especially when it comes to knowing God. Even people who are longtime believers fight upstream on this one. The first of the Ten Commandments, "You shall have no other gods before me," is both the most central to life and the hardest to follow. We simply don't want to see it his way.

Sixteenth-century Protestant reformer John Calvin argues that human beings are incurably religious. Everyone worships something. But human beings are also (curably) bent. Every group worships something different. Everyone's understanding of God is warped. Only God working his Word into somebody's outlook makes it possible for that person to know the true God. For Calvin, this confirms both the glory and the brokenness of humanity. We integrate irresistibly to a concept of God. Left to ourselves, in our bentness we produce mistaken integrations.

When it comes to the possibility of being wrong and being right, is knowing God any different from knowing your auto mechanic? Actually, given the bentness of our character to resist submission to God, we're more likely to get it wrong about God than we are to get it wrong about our auto mechanic.

The opening words of the Gospel of John are telling: "Through [Jesus, God the Word] all things were made; without him nothing was made that has been made. In him was life, and that life was the light of men. The light shines in the darkness, but the darkness has not understood it. . . . He was in the world, and though the world was made through him, the world did not recognize him." This says to me that humans have a huge epistemic problem. Imagine that we do not recognize the one who gives us life and light (that is, life-giving insight)! Not only are we inexplicably dense; we are also disastrously stuck in our density. But that is the point of the life-giving message of the good news of Jesus Christ. The one to whom we are resistantly blind is perfectly positioned to cure our blindness.

Nobody expects you to know a mechanic truly without doing the research. We shouldn't expect to know God without some effort either. Let the possibility of being mistaken drive us not to skepticism, but to passionate and determined learning, and to seeking wise guides. And may we also consider asking for help with the orientation of our hearts.

For Further Thought and Discussion

Give an example. Tell the story of a mistake you have made.

- How did you come to believe it in the first place?
- When did you come to recognize your mistake?
- How did you come to revise your truth claim?
- In retrospect, can you see that your mistaken claim was wholly or partly mistaken?
- Does your experience confirm or disconfirm this chapter's claims?
- How does understanding mistakes in this way serve to bring hope about knowing?

Consider etiquette. Given that people disagree about what is true, and that people make mistakes, what are some attitudes and responses that are appropriate and helpful for us to have toward ourselves and others?

Gauge your response to God. To what extent do you think all people are inclined to run away from God? To what extent do we run toward him? In what ways do these inclinations affect our knowing him truly?

21

"Are You the One Who Was to Come, or Should We Expect Someone Else?"

Responding to Doubts, Resolving to Believe

Okay, it's time for a reality check. I need to tell you, if you haven't guessed it already, that not every act of knowing feels like an "Oh! I see it!" moment. Not every conversion is a Damascus road experience. Nor does every math class end with a light bulb.

Sometimes the epistemic act feels more like a risky resolution, a dogged choice. It can feel that way at its beginning. It can also feel that way later, even after a glorious inception, on and off through the months and years of our holding and unfolding it.

■ Knowing as Dogged Choice

The surgeon reported that my husband's prostate tested positively for cancer. He advised removing it immediately. Imagine Jim's emotions that morning as he checked in for surgery. He felt perfectly healthy. On the strength of one

166

man's testimony and a couple of pathology reports, my husband was turning over his body to the invasion of a scalpel that would bring danger, pain, and a difficult, lengthy recovery. What an agonizingly risky epistemic act. It was hardly an "Oh! I see it!" moment!

Part of the personal contribution that supports an integration is just the knower's responsible decision that a pattern is present. Remember Sonarman Jonesy in The Hunt for Red October? He risked his reputation by divulging what sounded like a crazy hypothesis. Statisticians and scientists regularly assess whether the numerical correlation of the occurrence of two events should be taken to indicate the presence of a causal connection. Perhaps the statistical correlation comes in degrees. But our affirmation of truth on the basis of the statistics never is: we affirm a connection or we deny it.

The act of knowing involves the knower's active and responsible submission to reality. That definition articulates both of the essential features of human knowing: "responsible," and "submissive," active and passive. Every act of knowing has some portion of each, but their ratio may vary from truth claim to truth claim. It took a healthy dose of resolve on Jim's part to affirm the truth of the claim about his cancer. It would seem to involve little resolve to run from an oncoming tidal wave.

Life is full of such acts, some more difficult than others. In many life situations we do not have the leisure to suspend judgment pending better data. Not to decide is to decide. We have to push on in the face of something short of a glaringly obvious pattern because there is no other option. It calls for courageous resolve. And this courageous resolve, when proven true, merits the deep admiration of others. But that is only after the fact. Before the outcomes are fully revealed, the knower's act feels like risk, not recognition, resolution rather than some prophetic vision.

It is decidedly easier to trust the mechanic about your car than it is to trust the doctor about your body. It may be hardest of all to trust God enough to submit our life to him. But the point is that any act of knowing, of greater or of lesser import, can also be to a greater or lesser degree not a recognition but a resolution.

▌ Doubt and Resolve in the Life (and Death) of a Prophet

John, the cousin of Jesus, known as John the Baptist, had been called by God to announce the coming of the kingdom of God. He was granted the best of all "Oh! I see it!" moments when he heard a voice from heaven say to Jesus, "You are my Son, whom I love . . ." He knew himself to be God's designated prophet, his authoritative witness to Jesus' identity. He saw God use his words to change people's lives.

But John's fearless truthtelling provoked Herod, the tetrarch of Judea, to imprison him. Jesus' ministry progressed, but John was sidelined and facing death.

Doubts could not help but arise. If Jesus was who he said he was, would he not see to it that John was released? This didn't seem to be how it was supposed to happen when Messiah comes. Jesus himself had read from the prophets to the people assembled in the synagogue, "Proclaim liberty to the captives," and then had announced, "Today this has been fulfilled in your hearing"!

John sent a message to Jesus. "Are you the one who was to come, or should we expect someone else?" There could be no clearer expression of doubt, and no more reasonable ground for it. John was facing death, when he thought he had met the author of life itself.

Please note that this occurred after an "Oh! I see it!" moment. In our everyday holding of truth claims, we waver in our confidence. Even when the truth in question has knocked us over, there can come times when we must hold to the truth by firm resolve in the absence of ongoing manifestations of its reality.

Jesus sent a message back: "Go back and report to John what you have seen and heard: The blind receive sight, the lame walk, those who have leprosy are cured, the deaf hear, the dead are raised, and the good news is preached to the poor. Blessed is the man who does not fall away on account of me."

We are not told John's response. I'm sure these words were reassuring. But they could not possibly be exhaustive proof-positive. John may very well have ridden, not the reassurance, but the resolve, to his beheading.

The point of this chapter is that this is a legitimate shape for an act of knowing to take. It's okay to remain true to a belief even in the face of doubts and apparently contrary evidence. In fact, if the claim proves true, the resolve proves to have been an act of courage.

■ The Anatomy of Doubt

When holding, as we do, to the truth and reality of something or someone over a period of time, a knower can expect to move at times back and forth from being overwhelmed by the reality of his integration to feeling deserted by it. Even the act of knowing that had its inception in a blinding "Oh! I see it!" moment of recognition may come to call for risky resolve to maintain it in the face of apparent counterevidence. In those moments of felt desertion, moments of doubt, a knower holds on by teeth-clenching resolve. It isn't pretty or fun. But it is right to see that this is an appropriate part of the act of knowing.

The Hunt for Red October is one of my favorite movies, for it is the chronicling of a risky epistemic act. Military historian Jack Ryan believes against all opposition and odds that the Soviet commander of the nuclear submarine, Red October, is not starting World War III, but is, rather, defecting. His commitment to this belief drives Ryan through one risk after another in an effort to avert war and liberate Lieutenant Ramius. As he and a submarine crew prepare finally to board the Red October, Ryan is asked, "Are you sure?" and offered a pistol. Ryan pauses, sweating, pondering. With quiet resolution, he says, "He's defecting." A risky claim, born of recognition but now challenged in a moment of doubt. A dogged reaffirmation laced with courageous resolve.

Why, after even an initial "Oh! I see it!" moment, might doubts arise? Thinking of knowing as our reliance on clues to shape a pattern helps us unpack the causes of doubt. Just understanding this, I think, can be reassuring. Plus, it suggests how we might respond to doubts.

In St. Louis, Cardinal fans adore retired slugger Mark McGuire. And we just like the game. Baseball fans are quite familiar with, from the outside at least, the phenomenon known as a batting slump. It translates into a batter getting no hits over an abnormally and distressingly long number of games. I think a batting slump is, to the skill of baseball, what doubt is to belief.

One thing that causes doubt is reverting from focusing through clues to an integration to focusing on the clues on which we were relying. Knowing is actively integrating to a coherent focus through reliance upon subsidiary clues. What happens when we temporarily look back at the clues? We lose sight of the focus. All you need to do is blink, and the dolphins in the Magic Eye disappear.

It happens on the piano bench. I've watched my daughters in many musical performances. I remember one vividly. Seated at an exquisitely beautiful Baldwin on an elegant stage, before a select audience of parents, Stacey began cranking out a Scott Joplin rag with her usual confidence. Then she must have stopped and thought about what she usually never thought about: How do I figure out what the next note is? She was used to walking the tightrope, so to speak. But she started thinking about the safety net that wasn't there. She had lost her focus and was looking at the clues. Her playing ground to a distressing halt.

Actually, I think we can distinguish two doubt-producing movements in connection with the clues of our integrations. One is reverting to focus on the clues. The other, closely related one is feeling like, in our integration, that we're not in touch with our clues.

A pianist can grind to halt simply by looking at her fingers. Or she can grind to a halt, like Stacey did, by worrying that she didn't know what her fingers were doing. The first of these, I think, aligns with John's experience in prison. The second sounds to me like my student Michael's experience. Remember that he said that his answers concerning Christianity came to feel pat, and that he wondered why he said he believed it.

These two are closely related, obviously, but I feel it useful to distinguish them because I believe there are two ways to respond to doubts, and those responses, on the surface, appear to contradict each other. One is to try once more to look through the clues, reintegrate to the focus. The other is to take some time to look at the clues. In the end, I think that we cope by alternating these two movements, and that they are just the movements that make up good learning. Let me tell you what I mean.

First, we should try once more to look through the clues. We know enough about the act of knowing to see that it ought to feel uncomfortable to look back at the clues. When we look back at the particulars, we can feel that in themselves they don't account fully for the pattern that we have seen in them. Of course they don't, for it wasn't looking at them in themselves that prompted our integration; it was living in them and looking through them. To look at them is not to see the things on which our pattern was based. We access truth, and can only properly assess it, as we live in the pieces of the pattern as we do in our bodies. If looking at the pieces makes us feel doubtful, there's good reason for it: the pieces, without our living in them, aren't the starting point of our successful effort.

But we can take heart: the pattern that we have already glimpsed before came to us through those pieces once, and they did so most amazingly, the first time around when we had no solid idea what pattern we were looking for. So reintegration can happen. We can get inside the pieces another time. We need to struggle once more in the direction of the focus.

Did you ever have a moment when you stopped to think about how silly a certain letter or word is, when you look at it? Take the letter S, for example. Why on earth does a squiggle on a page prompt us to make a sound like a snake? Why not a sound like water? (What would a sound like water be?) Or the word jargon. Or giggle. Focusing on the actual word and its sound or its look makes us surprised that we could have thought it so transparent, that we could have been so easily "taken in." But we soon get over the odd feeling of the moment. We simply have to think again about the meaning of the word.

Often it takes more of a struggle to reintegrate the clues into the pattern. I think that knowing is a relationship between knower and known. In the act we promise to wait, as it were, to be blessed by that which we seek. Somehow, in our readdressing ourselves to the goal that we've temporarily lost sight of, we open ourselves afresh to its coming. Here is where resolve comes into play. Even in the face of doubt I can resolve to cling to the reality of the focus. And this resolve, like a marriage contract, opens the door to deeper relationship.

So, one remedy for doubt is to stop looking *at* the clues, striving again to look *through* them, to get back inside them. The other remedy appears opposite: it is to look *at* the clues—harder, and only for a time. Don't be afraid to do this, for when you do reachieve your focus, it will be a richer, more profound, confidence-producing experience. And this kind of clue scrutiny is the stuff of learning. It is a key way to develop our skill at accessing the world.

We are most familiar with this effort as plain old study and analysis, examining the underpinnings of our claims and actions to understand the what and how of the whole thing. Analysis is not all there is to knowing—identifying knowing with analysis, I believe, has been the central mistake of the modern model of knowledge. Clue scrutiny is not an end in itself, nor can it or should it be lifted out of the context of the larger picture that is knowing: humans engaging the world through patterns. But seeing analysis as a key instrument for the sake of a larger reintegration to a focus actually reinstates it, no longer as master, but more helpfully as servant.

Why is studying the clues valuable and important, if real knowing is living them, not looking at them? The clues that make up our integrations, you might say, are liable to get their feelings hurt if you forget them. They are happy being subsidiary, but you ignore them or take them for granted to your peril. We vector through them, but we never leave them behind. Perhaps the first time or times we integrated successfully, we got inside the clues and through them without knowing much about what we were doing. We sometimes have beginner's luck. But beginner's luck doesn't last. We are always better at our knowing if we embody our clues with a kind of sensitive intentionality that is often learned. Understanding this has profound implications for knowing, overcoming doubt, learning, and teaching.

What to do? First, give yourself to thinking through the clues. Scrutinize them. If you come to embrace them more deliberately, this can even open wider ranges of integration in the future. It's going to feel artificial, but it is also probably going to be temporary. Don't expect to stay with the particulars. Learn afresh to develop your subsidiary awareness of them.

The batting coach works with the batter in a slump, you can be sure. One thing they must do together is look at replays in slow motion. They may see that the batter has gotten into a bad habit of lifting a shoulder, for example. Then they go out to the batting cage, and the batter and the coach watch the batter's shoulder as he practices. Under the coach's guidance, the batter thinks through what it feels like from the inside to fix his shoulder. Then they start putting it back together.

Piano teachers have told my daughters: Don't stop thinking about what you are doing when you are practicing. Plan for what to do if autopilot fails you under pressure. Scrutinize your fingers and your fingering carefully in problem passages. Then put it back together. Stacey's current teacher, a seasoned accompanist, recently told her that brain studies on musicians show that young musicians have a well-developed artistic side of their brain. Mature musicians have that, and they also have a well-developed connection between the artistic and the analytical sides of their brain. What they did naturally at first by latent talent they now have analyzed to the point of being able to think their way through a performance. They are working artists, having successfully overcome stage fright. Don't be afraid of thinking about the clues and how they work.

In actuality, we move back and forth between both directions, from the clues, and to the clues, in any act of knowing over a period of time. We need to do both to know well. My church choir director drills us to make us sing our vowels properly. But on Sunday mornings, he says, "Forget everything I've taught you! Worship God!" In Wednesday rehearsals we analyze clues; on Sunday mornings we climb back into them as we reintegrate to our focus. Back and forth, back and forth.

Think about the message Jesus sent to John in light of what we have said about doubts. Jesus did not condemn John's doubts or signal that they were out of place. He met the concern with this two-fold response. He gave John a fresh look at the particulars of experience: the blind receive sight, the lame walk, those who have leprosy are cured, the deaf hear, the dead are raised, and the good news is preached to the poor. Plus, the particulars he gives are ones fraught with prophetic significance: this is just the sort of thing that will happen when God comes to his people. He was raising John's eyes afresh to the vision. The end of the ages was already inaugurated. It was underway. It was going to take time, but it was just a matter of time. "Blessed is the man who does not fall away on account of me."

John, in his resolve, no doubt continued to live in obedience to the reality of a Messiah whom he only knew in part. Obedience is a kind of attention to clues, and a kind of living in them, that reprompts the vision of the focus. And this kind of faithfulness is warranted. It is patient waiting in the darkness, clinging to the hope of truth.

Knowing happens. And doubts happen. Knowing can be recognition. Sometimes knowing takes resolve. But in admitting these things we accurately describe our epistemic experience and see a way to move forward. And we gather ground to hope.

■ Knowing Auto Mechanics and God: Doubt and Resolve as Part and Parcel of Knowing

Once again as I write, my old Taurus is headed for Jeff's shop. This time it's for inspection and to fix the two tail-lights I've managed to break. Suppose the car returns with my husband this afternoon, and the taillights are not fixed. How do I interpret that evidence? What if it were to lead me to wonder whether Jeff is there, or whether he is who he says he is, or whether he is a good mechanic? Suppose the word I get is that he has ordered the parts, and they won't be in until next week. I am quite reasonably left to trust his word in the absence of something I can see and hear. What's more, I have to. Even if I were to go to some other shop this minute, I would have the same trust-based wait, plus I would be dealing with someone new about whose character I had no clues. We never escape moments of resolve, at least in the car repair business. Along the way doubts can arise. I can meet these by thinking further about the clues which lead me to judge Jeff reliable. And I can reaffirm with him our mutual goal of keeping my Taurus safely on the road. I can resolve to trust that he will do his work well.

I do not see Jesus now. He told his disciples he was going to prepare a place for us and that when he returns, there will be no remaining question in anybody's mind that he is the supreme Lord and judge, the end of the ages. He calls us not to fall away in our belief. The Bible records story upon story of people who trusted God's words, both in moments of overwhelming recognition and on through moments, even years, of determined resolve.

The Bible calls this faith. We ought to be able to see by now that faith is a necessary ingredient of every single act of knowing, whether of auto mechanics or of God, whether in moments of recognition or in moments of resolve. It is the personal submitting of ourselves to the pattern we have shaped and recognized or chosen. It sustains our grasp on the pattern. It is our confi-

173

dence in the pattern. It doesn't oppose rationality; it is the oxygen that sustains rationality.

People who believe God, like John, experience doubt. They can stop and look at their fingers, focus on the apparently absent safety net. They can become frightened about the risk. If the act of knowing is as has been described, we can see also the mechanism of doubt.

We can meet our doubts with patience and hope. We can go back and scrutinize the particulars that undergird our integration with the expectation that fresh familiarity will prompt fresh and perhaps deeper integration. We can resolve to keep our eyes on the vision, the God whom we long to know. We can resolve to believe that he is who he says he is. In time the resolve is rewarded. Whoever comes to God, Scripture says, must believe that he is and that he rewards those who diligently seek him.

For Further Thought and Discussion

Give an example. What are some examples of statements you hold to be true, less out of overwhelming recognition, and more out of risky resolve? Do you think that these are equally legitimate responses? Why or why not?

Consider your experience of doubt. When have you experienced doubt, with respect to knowing God, or with respect to knowing anything else?

- Try to describe your doubt using the concepts presented in this chapter. For example, do you think your doubt involved looking back at the pieces of your experience, or did it involve overlooking the pieces of your experience?
- Or is there some other way you can relate your doubt to this model of the knowing process?
- How, in light of this chapter, should you respond to your doubt?
- How does this discussion help you feel about doubt and about the prospect about truth?

22

The Ethics of Knowing

Knowing as Interpersonal: Commitment, Respect, Patience, and Humility

Knowing as unlocking and engaging the real should suggest an appropriate attitude to accompany and enhance our knowing. It would be commitment, respect, patience, and humility.

Is knowing, in the final analysis, a matter of humankind milking its surroundings for everything they're worth, demanding answers for personal prosperity? Or is it a matter of humankind imposing on the unknown the truth that it arbitrarily chooses? Would either of these approaches work with someone you love? Neither of these even works in the lab. This suggests an ethic of knowing.

▋ Stalking Muskrats

In *Pilgrim at Tinker Creek*, Annie Dillard chronicles her laborious efforts to wait quietly and strategically for a glimpse of muskrats, which were profoundly rewarded. "In summer, I stalk," she says. "The creatures I seek have several senses and free will; it becomes apparent that they do not wish to be seen." She calls her stalking the *via negativa*. "When I stalk this way I take my stand on a bridge and wait, emptied. I put myself in the way of the creature's passage." Dillard says, "I found out the hard way that waiting is better than pursuing." Stalking requires surrender of self-consciousness, she notes. "It used to bother me . . . ; I just could not bear to lose so much dignity that I would completely alter my whole way of being for a muskrat. So I would move or look around or scratch my nose, and no muskrats would show, leaving me alone with my dignity for days on end, until I decided that it was worth my while to learn—from the muskrats themselves—how to stalk."

"Stalking is a pure form of skill, like pitching or playing chess. Rarely is luck involved. I do it right or I do it wrong; the muskrat will tell me, and that right early. . . . Can I stay still? How still? It is astonishing how many people cannot, or will not, hold still."

She is quick to draw the analogy to Heisenberg's uncertainty principle. "The electron is a muskrat; it cannot be perfectly stalked. And nature is a fan dancer born with a fan; you can wrestle her down, throw her on the stage and grapple with her for the fan with all your might, but it will never quit her grip. She comes that way; the fan is attached." Newtonian physics led us to believe, she notes, that "we remove the veils one by one, painstakingly, adding knowledge to knowledge and whisking away veil after veil, until at last we reveal the nub of things, the sparkling equation from whom all blessings flow." Now, Dillard says with Eddington and other "mystical physicists," no clear distinction remains between the Natural and the Supernatural.

Another connection: Dillard quotes Moses begging God to show him his glory. Even God likes to hide. "Just a glimpse, Moses: a cliff in the rock here, a mountaintop there, and the rest is denial and longing. You have to stalk everything. Everything scatters and gathers; everything comes and goes like fish under a bridge."

But "the news, after all, is not that muskrats are wary, but that they can be seen. The hem of the robe was a Nobel prize to Heisenberg; he did not go home in disgust. I wait on the bridges and stalk along banks for those moments I cannot predict, when a wave begins to surge under the water. . . . 'Surely the Lord is in this place; and I knew it not.' The fleeing shreds I see, the back parts, are a gift, an abundance. When Moses came down from the cliff in Mount Sinai, the people were afraid of him: the very skin on his face shone."

■ How Knowing Is like a Marriage

"The lover can see, and the knowledgeable," she says. If the kind of knowing we aspired to as "hard science" was *impersonal*, pursuing an agenda of stripping bare the most basic intricacies of the world, the kind of knowing Annie Dillard describes is *interpersonal*, which uncovers even more deeply and precisely because it respects the mystery. Which one of these pictures prevails, I think, profoundly affects how we approach the enterprise and what comes of it. I think it profoundly affects and is affected by how we see ourselves and our role in this world.

I would like to suggest that knowing is more like an unfolding friendship anchored in a pledge or covenant, a marriage. We can profitably compare the act of knowing to a wedding ceremony. In such a relationship, your part is only ever half. There is another partner, and thus a mutuality, which to overlook would spell disaster. Each partner sweats to think of the risk and the commitment that the pledge calls for; each one beams with joy at the prospects of the realities to be discovered. Without the pledge, the realities are not to be had. But in light of the prospect of engaging the real, such commitment is delightful.

Similarly, I think it helps to see the interresponsive nature of knowing. The knower is a person, and the known is personlike in its responsiveness according to the ways of the knower, and in having a mind and mystery of its own. The knower is only ever half. And the knower must expect to cultivate the relationship, if knowing is to reach its full range of possibilities.

In the marriage vows two people make to each other we see both the active responsibility and the delighted submission that make up the epistemic act. When it comes to knowing, it just doesn't happen without a responsibly resolved commitment of ourselves. Knowing takes submission to the known, stalking—waiting, emptied—for muskrats, meeting them on their terms. Knowing takes commitment to that which is yet to be discovered, a kind of pledge of good faith. The lover can see, is permitted to see. The seeing only ever follows and responds to the wanting, the longing, the personal, self-giving pledge. It takes refusing to scratch your nose.

Knowing unfolds, as does a relationship, through time. Acts of coming to know are forever paradigmatic, for mystery remains an element to the core. Never is the experiment exhaustively over. But for a relationship to unfold in this way, a pledge must undergird it. A covenant can and must extend through time. It extends through times of delight and times of doubt. It calls for determined and unwavering faithfulness to a vision. And the growth of truth-based knowledge requires this and the patient respect that accompanies it.

But even in the context of a pledge, knowing cannot be forced. The known "has free will," as Dillard says: you cannot force its response. It calls for patience. It calls for reverence, respect.

Humility is called for as well. I am not the god of reality. I don't make it all happen the way I want. I am a partner. And as a partner, I can't demand compliance and answers. Nor can I make reality what I want it to be. What's more, I might, along the way, be mistaken or partly mistaken. Humility is an appropriate virtue for knowers who might be mistaken.

And as with a friendship or a marriage, so it is in the relationship we call knowing: commitment, humility, respect, and patience access realities untouchable via impatient demands. What we can't demand, we can wait for with hope. For these qualities reveal the knower's longing, our belief that the wait is worth it, that the reality we seek to know is significant. You can't rush reality. But neither can you resist it. Reality opens itself to those who trust it. "Surely the Lord was in this place, and I knew it not."

We need to learn to live with this kind of reverence. The traditional model of knowing, the product of centuries of searching for exhaustive certainty, eventually stripped us not only of the confidence we should have regarding engaging the real, but also of the reverence that it requires and deserves.

From time to time we need to be reminded that we need to treat people whom we wish to know with respect, that revelations come within covenantal relationships of respect, patience, and humility. With people, our inappropriate arrogance can be met by a left hook or by stony silence. People hide themselves from arrogant demands, but open themselves to humble requests.

But the larger oversight may be what we do with electrons and muskrats. I do not think that we typically think about respect and patience and humility when it comes to knowing muskrats, or making other discoveries about the world. Often we have helped ourselves to reality's treasures before taking the time to explore further dimensions and consequences. Often we have forgotten that there is so much more, hidden horizons, easy to miss on a cursory sweep. We have forgotten the respect and patience and humility that learning and unlocking the world requires. But this is what Dillard and others call us to. And it is what good scientists know firsthand.

▮ Knowing Auto Mechanics and God: Exercising Virtues That Enhance the Relationship

When it comes to my relationship with my auto mechanic, my respect for his reliability actually serves to enhance his reliability. Were I to demand instant and total satisfaction, our working relationship would be damaged. His discouragement concerning pleasing his customer might prompt halfhearted efforts and increase careless mistakes.

When it comes to my relationship with God, my respect for who he is actually serves to enhance my knowing him. In fact, I simply cannot know him if I refuse to submit in reverence to him. The Bible makes it plain that obedience leads a person further into truth. Nor, even within a relationship of respect and trust, can I expect to have every question answered or request granted instantaneously and as described. In fact, the Bible, even as it offers plenty of evidence that God is steadfastly good to his people, also summons us to trust that God is good even in times of heartbreak and suffering. Humility, respect, and patience are most commonly thought of as Christian virtues. What has been less obvious to us is that they apply favorably to all acts of knowing, even of muskrats and of auto mechanics. The thing to learn in this chapter, then, may be not so much about God, and more about muskrats and auto mechanics. But the parity of the two heightens our prospects for knowing God.

I think that the world that is the object of our knowing has personal characteristics, responds to our knowing, has this free will Dillard speaks of, unfolds in surprising but recognizably charactered possibilities, precisely because it reflects the personhood and character of God its creator. One of the many astounding things that Jesus says is, "I am the truth" (John 14:6). If truth is ultimately a person to be known, then it is reasonable to think that knowing truth should work like knowing a person. In fact, the way Scripture presents God and our knowing him is as a lover, a husband to his people, whom to know involves an interpersonal, unfolding, covenantal relationship. Knowing God is a relationship that deserves to be front and center in our lives for a number of obvious reasons. I suggest that this chapter shows that the covenant relationship should, additionally, be taken to be front and center in our understanding of knowing. The covenant mutuality of God and his people is paradigmatic for all human knowing. Knowing is like that: interpersonal, pledge-based, calling for respect and humility and patience.

If we understood this more fully, we would fulfill more appropriately the role that Scripture says is given to humans with respect to the world, a role aptly described as *stewardship*. If knowing is as I have described it here, then knowing just is the stewardship, the responsible care and cultivation of the earth that is our calling and our identity as humans. It is the very thing we were made to do. Knowing is something people do with reality. It grows naturally out of our situatedness in the world, it vectors us toward the world, it shapes the world even as it responds to it. Good, responsible knowing brings blessing, shalom; irresponsible knowing brings curse. In doing this well, Scripture says we image God, much as Simba, the young Lion King, imaged his father in ruling well.

There is much, much to think about here! So much promise, so much dignity, so much delight. When we think of knowing in this way, we are not too far removed from worship.

For Further Thought and Discussion

Consider your approach.

- Name some of your own acts of knowing in which you now see that you exercised commitment, respect, humility, or patience, and did so to advantage.
- Can you think of some other times when you neglected these, and did so to disadvantage?

Reflect on knowing God. In what ways does this discussion influence your thoughts about knowing God?

23

Confidence and Hope

The Rich Dividends of a Fresh Approach to Understanding Knowing

I hope that by now, having read this far, you feel within you a sea change that you might label *hope*. Whether or not this is something you already are starting to sense, it will be helpful to put it into words.

Simply put: On a model that required certainty, certainty ended up dying, and little hope seemed to remain for knowing anything, let alone knowing God. An extended look at ordinary human experience in knowing has helped us to see that knowing happens, to see how it works, and to see how we can reasonably hope by means of it to access the real.

The misguided quest for certainty was in the end the very thing that blinded us to the substantial grounds we have for confidence in our efforts to engage the world. We cannot be exhaustively certain; nor would we want to pay its price. The alternative to what is in fact sterile certainty is a very fertile capacity to engage and evoke reality. We need not mourn its demise when *confidence* waits in the wings to replace it. And confidence is a concept that accords better, and not only with the risky efforts of our ventures. It also accords better with the prospect of their success. It restores hope.

Let's be specific about our fresh hope. How does seeing how human knowing works restore hope? First, we can be hopeful about our accessing the real. We embody it, and we extend ourselves into it as we engage it. Of course this cannot be fully captured in words! We see now that when we are encouraged to accredit more-than-verbal knowing, we find ourselves immersed in an undeniable awareness of the real. We live the real. And this living is knowing, and the necessary and profound roots of all the truth claims we put into words.

Because we are human, our lived knowing issues in language. Again, we have fresh cause for hope. For while words and concepts, if inappropriately articulated or applied, hinder our grasp of the real, apt words and concepts are so many tools that extend our hold on the world, keys that unlock fresh vistas of possibilities. Words, like works of art, work evocatively as much as they do representatively. In addition to our always knowing more than we can tell, we are also always *saying more* than we consciously realize. We have fresh hope because we have restored to us the possibility of being proved right in our knowing (along with the possibility of being wrong!).

A realistic sense of ourselves, of our capacities as knowers, restores hope. Greater significance, responsibility, and even freedom are to be felt as we accurately sense and extend our fit with the world. We have learned that there is a human, bodily rooted, future-oriented, truth-loving way of knowing. We've learned to recognize how it feels from the inside. We've learned to appreciate our strategic situatedness that opens the world to us. We've learned to access the real by cultivating our rootedness in it.

By contrast, the kind of freedom implied by the thought that we humans completely determine our reality leaves us with a gnawing sense of the relative insignificance of our choices. I think it leads not to total responsibility but to careless irresponsibility, both with regard to ourselves and with regard to other humans, not to mention to the world. And, paradoxically, it leads not to a deeper sense of identity and dignity but to a disheartening lack of it. Humans were not made to be God. The attempt doesn't in the end feel like a fit.

I heard someone tell this story: he was leading a discussion with a group of high school students. He asked, "How many of you here believe that you can grow up to be anything you want to be?" Several raised their hands. "How many of you think you could be a star professional basketball player?" One hand went up. It belonged to a girl who was four-feet-ten. The leader responded, "You may be the only one in the room that thinks that!" In holding out for the possibility of doing anything she wanted, the young woman was probably overlooking the way she was uniquely and strategically gifted to engage the world.

In *Ever After*, a movie version of the Cinderella story, Prince Henry finally comes to his senses. His mother and the woman he has come to love have both said to him: "You were born to privilege, and with it comes specific obligation." He has to this point felt only the weighty chains that his birthright put on his personal freedom. But now he says something like this: "I used to think that if I cared about anything, I would have to care about everything, and I would go stark raving mad! But now I have found my purpose. . . . And I feel . . . the most wonderful . . . freedom." Similarly, understanding the privilege and obligation of our situatedness as knowers brings hope, purpose, and even freedom—freedom from slavery to a misguided expectation of ourselves as knowers.

Recognizing that knowing is a skill also restores hope about ourselves. Knowing calls for us to develop our latent abilities, to embrace the struggle it takes to pursue truth. It calls us to accredit our growing knack of getting it right.

Knowing, I sometimes think, is like snowboarding. (You, like me, may have no firsthand experience of snowboarding! Think of something you do that you consider a risky challenge that is fun. For me, it is writing and teaching.) The point is this: The better your skill at it, the more you love embracing the risk. Your love is born out of your confidence in your own well-developed skill. You might get it wrong, but not only your frequency at getting it right but also the inward feel of the aptness of your efforts bring joy. Baseball fans adore well-fielded balls. We love watching a fielder hurtle through the air to nab an impossible line drive. On the television replay you can often see that the fielder loves it too. He lives for that moment.

In knowing, we are restored to being confident navigators among the clues of our lives. We have a sense of them that we cannot put into words, which nevertheless guides us in our quest. We are now freed to accredit this sense, and thus free intentionally to rely on it. We are like bats and whales, continually and confidently orienting ourselves as we pursue our conjectures into the world.

So hope and confidence are restored for us in reference to the real, and in reference to ourselves. Hope is also restored when it comes to trusting authoritative guides. In this book, we have also talked about the profoundly critical role of the guiding word in every act of knowing. Always there is an authoritative word, either external to us or gradually embodied by us, as we move forward in our knowing. We engage the real only through submission to its guidance. About the credibility and correctness or our particular authority we can be wrong, even as we can be wrong both about the real and about ourselves. With regard to all three we must continually be assessing and making course corrections. But as our skill grows, so grows our confidence: we can be wrong, but we can also be right.

When it comes to the authoritative word, we never have the option of total withholding of trust from all authoritative guides. Total rejection of authority is an illusion. This is something that philosophers of the modern period, beginning with Descartes, failed to recognize. If you reject all others' authority, you have no choice but to submit to your own. And all of us know by experience that at least at some critical times in our lives, submitting to our own authority has proven a disastrous mistake.

Sadly, we can be like the Dwarfs in C. S. Lewis's *The Last Battle*, who, having been taken once, refused to believe the truth. Sadder still, philosophers have, I think, brought disgrace on the discipline by glorifying the categorical rejection of authority, just like those Dwarfs. "We're on our own now. No more Aslan, no more kings, no more silly stories about other worlds. The Dwarfs are for the Dwarfs." As they sit in their circle facing each other and chanting in what they think is a filthy stable, they fail to see the new Narnia unfolding around them, because of their unbelief. Aslan's verdict on the Dwarfs "refusing to be taken in": "You see, they will not let us help them. They have chosen cunning instead of belief. Their prison is only in their own minds, yet they are in that prison; and so afraid of being taken in that they can not be taken out. But come, children. I have other work to do."

We cannot avoid the choice. We can avoid a poor choice. Compare it to signing up for courses at the university. Would you purposely choose a bad teacher if you knew and could choose otherwise? And no matter what the class, will you learn anything new if you do not trust yourself to the teacher's (or the text's) guidance? Perhaps such trust feels like exposing our flank, admitting to vulnerability, taking a risk. So be it. A hurtling outfielder in pursuit of a ball cannot but expose his flank. Nor can the serious pursuer of the real. But our submission is never blind or rigid. It breathes and moves with our effort.

But having recognized the role of authoritative words in our acts of knowing, we have fresh hope of our well-placed confidence in them, fresh hope of their power to guide us to the real. It gives us the courage to scrutinize and steward our trust as we navigate the world.

▌ Being on the Way to Knowing

This new way of thinking has helped us along the way to resolving some puzzles and reuniting some domains divorced in the wake of our traditional concept of knowledge. I personally have felt the lovely resolution of reuniting the ivory tower with the world of everyday human experience, seeing the jewels of the one return to the streets of the other, where they belong. The new model moves us to reunite knowing and doing, fact and value, discovery and confirmation, art and science, faith and reason, and mind and body. It points out the way between the Scylla and Charybdis of modernism and postmodernism. It heightens our sense of our character and value as humans. And it removes some of the unnecessary hurdles we encountered in coming to know God.

It helps us see that the risky placing of confidence in God that Scripture calls "belief," the orienting of our whole lives toward him, just is the epistemic act, the ordinary act of knowing that we replicate repeatedly in weaving the tapestry of our lives. Knowing God is like knowing your auto mechanic. We can and do know our auto mechanic. Therefore, we can and do know God.

A final word about hope. Hope necessarily implies a patient but confident wait for future developments. This model of knowing teaches us what we already knew by experience: truth takes time, but truth is worth pursuing, and truth is worth the wait. Just because we don't get it now, or don't see it all now, no longer requires us to concede that we do not *know*, that we are not involved in an act of knowing. Knowing vectors us into the world, and it also vectors us through time. Call it "being on the way to knowing" if you like. Knowing is a longing, a leaning into the world, with a patient but confident expectation of reward. We already know in our lives what it is to rejoice in the propects of something not yet fully known. (Christmas presents, anyone?) Now we have learned to consider this a legitimate part of the epistemic act. We rejoice in the hope of truth. This buys us the freedom and the right to wait.

The best wedding I ever attended was that of Julie and Frank. Julie was a TV producer, and a knockout brunette. Frank had just landed a strategic job with the State Department. The preacher's sermon was inspiring. But the best moment came after the kiss, when the bride, in her fabulous soprano voice, sang John Rutter's "The Lord Bless You and Keep You"—first to her groom, and then to the assembled witnesses. It was a moment of glory.

I'm told that the night before was, by contrast, rather tense. Frank had not appeared. Julie's sister had spent the week with her in joyous preparation. "When is Frank coming?" Julie's sister would ask. She had not met Frank. Julie would reply, "He's coming!" Friday evening came, and the wedding rehearsal. Frank was not there. "So where's Frank?" her sister said. "He's coming!" Julie persisted with a smile. They rehearsed without the groom. On they went to a sumptuous rehearsal dinner. Frank was not there. Julie's sister, pressed to exasperation, said, "Julie! I don't believe Frank exists!" To which Julie replied doggedly, "He's coming!"

At about 9:30, Julie went to the doors of the banquet room and opened them wide. In walked Frank, into the room and into her waiting arms. The groom had come, straight from the airport, and straight from Washington, D.C. It was worth the wait. And the bride was proven right.

■ Knowing Auto Mechanics and God: "Follow Me"

Knowing is often like waiting for Frank. Obviously, I don't get weepy-eyed at the glory of waiting for my car to be fixed. But it still involves hope, the hope of truth. I told you that I sent my old Taurus in for inspection. And I've told you how I have lived with the clunking that was caused by its weakened struts. Jeff had refrained from fixing them, to save unnecessary expense. I have to say, I was growing so tired of the clunking that I had considered asking for new struts for my birthday.

The day after the inspection, I set out to drive to the grocery store. I was immediately overcome with the most delicious sensation of buoyancy! No more clunk! "What happened?" I asked on the phone when I got home. "The struts were broken this time. The car wouldn't have passed inspection without new ones." My belief in Jeff's reliability holds a continuous promise for the future. This time it issued in noticeably delightful driving. It also issued in a checkbook divot. I believe my claim that he is a reliable mechanic is true; a good portion of that is perhaps better expressed as a hope of truth.

But well-placed hope does not disappoint us. It is not certainty, but it is perhaps the more delicious for its anticipation. We rejoice in the prospect of knowing.

Already converted Christians are still coming to know God. This is an epistemic act in process. The believer's experience is still, profoundly, "not yet." Jesus' first coming was the beginning of God's final initiative in the world. To understand it truly is to grasp its inherent connection with a second, final return. And Jesus promised to return. "Now we see in part but then we shall know as we already are known." "Not having seen him, we love him." We "love his appearing." These are the Bible's words. Scripture records numerous prayers of the apostles that the believers they encouraged would know Christ better. It deserves to be called *hope.*

Our knowing God is rightly seen to be a confidence placed not in our epistemic efforts, but in the character of the one we have come to know. Consider the poignant and passionate words of the apostle Paul, written in the dungeon under the Roman Forum, on the eve of his execution: "Yet I am not ashamed, because *I know whom I have believed,* and am convinced that he is able to guard what I have entrusted to him for that day."

Lesslie Newbigin ends his profound little book, *Proper Confidence,* with these words: "The confidence proper to a Christian is not the confidence of one who claims possession of demonstrable and indubitable knowledge. It is the confidence of one who has heard and answered the call that comes from the God through whom and for whom all things were made: 'Follow me.'"

Christians wait in expectation for God's coming, as Annie Dillard waited for the muskrat, as Julie waited confidently for Frank. We know it to be risky. We might be wrong. But as acts of knowing go, this is a bona fide sample. Knowing about knowing undergirds our hope.

For Further Thought and Discussion

Assess your own hope and confidence.

- How has this book affected your level of hope and confidence with regard to knowing?
- How has this book affected your level of hope and confidence with regard to knowing God?
- What lingering questions and concerns do you have?

24

The Rest of Michael's Story
Knowing Knowing, Knowing God

I told you at the outset about Michael, one of my students, who was wrestling with deep questions about knowing. Having become a Christian at fifteen, having seen God's work in his life to change him, and having begun graduate theological studies, Michael's professed claims about Christianity came to feel pat. He was no longer sure of what he believed. He was wrestling, in particular, with trusting God's goodness and power in the face of evil, and with the fact that he lacked certainty in what he believed.

While he was working as a janitor, he had time to think, and, when he could, to try to pray. "In those quiet times, I went back over what I had believed all along, piece by piece. I scrutinized the particulars of my life. I was reading Peter Kreeft's *Making Sense of Suffering*. One thing he said in there made a good deal of sense to me. He said that when a suffering child cries out to his father, he is asking not so much for an explanation as he is for reassurance.

"I decided to do the same—to ask God for reassurance. And I think that is just what began to happen: God began to reassure me. My existential angst began to dissipate. I began to believe God again, and to pray."

But while he felt fresh reassurance as to God's goodness, the epistemological questions didn't go away. "It was like I was starting to see some light at the edge of a dark forest, but I was nowhere near being out of the forest yet. I felt as if I could know, but I didn't know how to talk about knowing. I had been reassured of God's goodness, but that assurance felt shaky. I wondered whether it would stand against the waves of doubt breaking on the shore of my life."

Michael returned to seminary. In a class on epistemology, his story and mine intersected and began to interweave. He heard what I have described to you in this book. Coming to grasp this model of knowing, he began to make fresh sense of his experience. It prompted a fresh integration of the clues of his life to a profounder focal awareness.

"I came to see how much my struggles had to do with certainty. I came to see that it's okay to have confidence, and right not to have certainty. Certainty is an illusion. Confidence is right. And doubting is not the same as unbelief. When I thought about all my experiences knowing—knowing God, or knowing anything—I saw that I had been pursuing certainty, but all along I had really been living out confidence. The fact that I couldn't get, in my knowing, beyond the possibility of doubt to arrive at some standard of certainty had caused me to render my life experiences invalid. That's why the answers had come to feel pat—my answers constantly fell short of the ideal of certainty. But I came to see that I could offer answers with confidence; it was an act of integrity, not to wait for certainty, but to speak with confidence of the coherent patterns of my life, even though I might be mistaken. I regained the ability to articulate why I believe in Christ.

"When I came to understand that I could be confident in my knowing, and to grasp how the act of knowing happens, it validated my experience, not just of faith, but of all knowing. Understanding the act of knowing reinvigorated for me the whole process of knowing and learning. It was like a Copernican revolution, a huge worldview shift for me. It has come to affect all of my knowing and learning, and so all of my living.

"And it keeps going. I keep seeing fresh implications and possibilities of this model. Recently, for example, I've been thinking in light of it what Scripture means when it tells us to 'fix our eyes on Jesus.' And I've been thinking about what the model of knowing implies for worship. The future possibilities seem endless. It's real.

"Now I have hope of truth, even though I don't feel I have all the answers. I have a direction in which to proceed. And I have peace."

Michael is on his way to the African country of Ghana, to help pastors there receive the seminary training that has not in the past been available to them. One day, in the intervening weeks between his recent graduation and his departure, I encountered him and asked him how he was. Times were not that easy:

it's difficult to reorient to life after graduation. He was waiting tables at a restaurant, and trying to raise funding for his trip. But his next words complete his story: "But my times with the Lord have been very rich and sweet. God is real."

Michael's experience replicates my own, and thus becomes part of my own integrated pattern. I know God as I see him at work in Michael's life. It is awesome and humbling. I have the sense that before Michael and I entered the room, so to speak, God was there, watching us, and working. And both of us also sense the reality of this pattern of knowing, as we anticipate the prospect of an array of future possibilities, not only in our own lives, but in the lives of others who read this book. Perhaps yours will be one of them.

I have the privilege of seeing my students' faces relax into smiles as they start to grasp what they are hearing. They thought they wanted certainty and couldn't have it. They come to see that confidence is not simply a legitimate alternative, but the only alternative, and a preferred one at that. Having come to understand, they learn to delight in the prospects. Why would you ever feel like you had settled for something less? Why would you cower in the ski lodge if you could cultivate and revel in the skill of alpine downhill? Life is opened and restored to them.

We learn to hold what we believe to be true with confidence, with the humility that comes from knowing we might be wrong or we might not have this opportunity to access the world, and with the tantalizing prospect of uncovering more, with the courage to be patient as one is in a relationship. We learn to engage in the hard but hopeful work of pursuing the truth. This is true about knowing auto mechanics and copperheads, solving cryptograms and Magic Eyes, reading Chinese, finding out what went bump in the night, playing peek-a-boo, laying out for a line drive, discovering the Northwest Passage.

And it's also true about knowing God. Last Easter, my church's choir did not simply repeat the Nicene Creed; we *sang* Mozart's setting of it, and we sang it from our toes. I professed with humbly confident and risky abandon that I believe those claims to be true. Knowing knowing liberates us from the epistemic straitjacket that kept us from such confident acclamation. It frees us to the risky and heady joy of knowing, trusting, and obeying God as real.

For Further Thought and Discussion

Think about handling doubt.

- How did some of Michael's responses exemplify the advice, given in chapter 20, for coping with doubt?

- In what ways did he scrutinize the particulars?
- In what ways did he address himself afresh to the integrative vision of God?

Consider confidence. How did coming to understand confidence rather than certainty as the proper goal of knowing affect Michael? How does this realization affect you?

Write the next installment of your story. How is your story developing? Since you last told your story of knowing, has there been a fresh installment? Tell that chapter now. What advice would you now give to people struggling with questions about knowing?

25

Known by God

A Double-take Look at the Power of the Pattern

I have in my mind a picture. I imagine I have been marooned on a tropical island. I wake up on the beach and start inland to explore. I plod through steamy jungles. I pick my way up a gradual rise in terrain. I stop to catch a breath and look farther ahead. The dense jungle is opening slightly to allow light from beyond the trees to reach me. I look first at the pattern of trees interspersed by light. But my eyes are suddenly drawn to a different, further pattern. Beyond and between the trees, I gradually become aware, I am looking into a pair of enormously, fantastically large . . . EYES! Judging by their distance from each other, and their size at the distance they are from me, I surmise their owner is the size of the Sphinx. And those eyes are looking at *me*.

What I imagine is an act of coming to know. But when all is said and done, its defining feature is that it is *an act of coming to be known*. And a terrifying one at that. Think of how fear would rise physically into your throat if you were doing the seeing! In the success of my knowing, the tables are radically turned. I am no longer calling any shots. I am no longer the one asking the questions. Whatever questions I had now seem ludicrous. Their being answered or not seems inconsequential. I am called upon to answer for myself. I am utterly at the mercy of a living being, a being who has noticed me. There is no escaping. I have been known. It is no longer me shaping the world. I face the inquiries of someone else, and their initiatives; I fear complete extinction.

All through *The Hunt for Red October,* military historian Jack Ryan has passionately pursued a man he hardly knows, the famous Lieutenant Ramius. Near the end of the movie, the moment comes when Ryan boards the *Red October* and meets him face to face. Ryan's knowing Ramius is met by Ramius's interrogating him! First it is "How did you know I was defecting?" Then it is, in the face of destruction, "Steer this ship, do as I tell you, trust me and not your ranking officer!" Then it is "What books did you write? I know this book! Your conclusions were all wrong!" (Before the historian knew the commander, the commander had known the historian.) Then it is something to the effect of "Shoot the bad guy, but don't hurt the equipment." Knowing Ramius propels Ryan into a rather ruthless relationship. In retrospect, I think Ryan would say the terror of being known is worth it.

Acts of knowing can be like that. We shape our integrative pattern and unlock the door. We find ourselves in the presence of a presence. We are relating to a center of agency outside ourselves. If this agent is personal, we can feel that we are no longer the one asking the questions.

The experience of knowing God, we can find, turns into the experience of being known by God. In the words of an old hymn—

> I sought the Lord, and afterward I knew
> He moved my soul to seek him, seeking me;
> It was not I that found, O Savior true; no, I was found of thee.

Being found by God, for the Christian, proves to be a profoundly sweet experience. But we would be remiss to forget the terror.

The Bible records accounts of various people who met God. We've already talked about some of Jesus' contemporaries meeting him. Here's one of my favorite stories. It's a favorite because I love the logic. But my point at the moment is the terror. "The angel of the LORD," an Old Testament reference to an appearance of God himself, comes to the parents of the yet-to-be-born Samson, Manoah and his wife. He promises Samson's birth to the currently sterile wife, tells them how to raise him, and promises that Samson will deliver the oppressed clans of Israel. Manoah does not at first realize that he is speaking with God. Manoah offers food to the visitor. The angel of the Lord declines, and tells him instead to offer a sacrifice to the God of Israel. Manoah complies. Here's what happens:

As the flame blazed up from the altar toward heaven, the angel of the LORD ascended in the flame. Seeing this, Manoah and his wife fell with their faces to the ground. When the angel of the LORD did not show himself again to Manoah and his wife, Manoah realized that it was the angel of the LORD.

"We are doomed to die!" he said to his wife. "We have seen God!"

But his wife answered, "If the LORD had meant to kill us, he would not have accepted a burnt offering and grain offering from our hands, nor shown us all these things or now told us this."

The woman gave birth to a boy and named him Samson.

Coming to be known by God can be terrifying.

In another place, the prophet Isaiah reports a vision of God in his temple, with huge angels proclaiming his holiness, and the pillars shaking and the room filled with smoke. "Woe to me!" he cries. "I am ruined! For I am a man of unclean lips, and I live among a people of unclean lips, and my eyes have seen the King, the LORD Almighty."

All through the story of Job, the agonized man begs for God to present himself that he might question him about his suffering despite his faithful obedience. His request is granted—in part. God comes, but Job is not the one who asks the questions:

> Then the LORD answered Job out of the storm.
> He said:
> "Who is this that darkens my counsel with words without knowledge?
> Brace yourself like a man;
> > I will question you,
> > and you shall answer me.
> "Where were you when I laid the earth's foundation?"

The heavenly harangue continues for four chapters. A humbled Job responds:

> You asked, "Who is this that obscures my counsel without knowledge?"
> > Surely I spoke of things I did not understand,
> > things too wonderful for me to know.
> You said, "Listen now, and I will speak;
> > I will question you,
> > and you shall answer me."
> My ears had heard of you
> > but now my eyes have seen you.
> Therefore I despise myself
> > and repent in dust and ashes.

194

Job's questions are trumped. The tables are turned. Their "answer" consists in the powerful presence of the God who formed the world, and who now queries Job.

Some Galilean fishermen have had a totally unprofitable night. A carpenter's son who has begun teaching groups of people at the water's edge turns to them and says, "Put out into deep water, and let down the nets for a catch." Of all the nerve! Who is this guy? Simon Peter decides to humor him: "Master, we've worked hard all night and haven't caught anything. But because you say so, I will let down the nets."

His sarcasm is met with so large a catch of fish that the nets begin to break. And suddenly, the questioner finds himself the questioned. Peter falls at Jesus' knees and says, "Go away from me, Lord; I am a sinful man!"

One more story. Jesus and his disciples are crossing the Sea of Galilee in a boat. Jesus is asleep. A furious squall comes up, bad enough to terrorize seasoned fishermen. They wake Jesus and demand: "Teacher, don't you care if we drown?"

Jesus "got up, rebuked the wind and said to the waves, 'Quiet! Be still!' Then the wind died down and it was completely calm."

Put yourself in the disciples' shoes. Which is the greater terror—an unbeatable storm, or a person who calms it with a spoken word? These fishermen "were terrified and asked each other, 'Who is this? Even the wind and the waves obey him!' "

People who have truly known God will have lived through terror—terror at the thought of who he is, and terror at the thought of being utterly at his mercy. The terror lies not so much in the knowing as in the being known. Aptly the psalmist expresses the feeling: "Look away from me, that I may rejoice again before I depart and am no more."

The gaze of God is both what we fear and what we can't do without. Scripture makes it clear that apart from God's coming to us and opening our eyes, we cannot know him truly. Talk about epistemic difficulties! For us to know him, he must know us first. Our knowing is warped, especially when it comes to knowing God, because of human rebellion against God. There is something inside us that doesn't want to know him, even as another part of us does. Our blindness thus requires the terror of his meeting us.

What does God do for our knowing? I believe that he meets us at three points in our act of knowing. You can already guess the triad I have in mind! God meets us in the Word: Scripture is God's authoritatively guiding us to truth about himself, ourselves, and his world. God meets us in the world: not only does the world offer glimpses of his glory and of his mind, but Jesus came into space and time, inaugurating restoration through his life, death, and resurrection. And God meets us within ourselves, as God the Holy Spirit is the one who can and must open our eyes for us to be able to grasp truth.

Actually, I think God is involved not just in our knowing him, but in our knowing anything at all—auto mechanics, copperheads, golf swings, Spanish, and the Pythagorean theorem. When knowing happens and the world is truthfully engaged, God has been at work. The integrative act is very much a human struggle. But we know full well the struggle never guarantees the result. Even for the highly skilled, the knower finds himself or herself humbled by the mystery and blessing of a coherent pattern no antecedents could fully determine. The pattern meets us. This is, profoundly, God's world.

People whom God knows rightly experience terror. But people cauterized by the coals of such an encounter also know the blessing of his steadfast love. Manoah and his wife receive a longed-for son and deliverer. Isaiah receives healing and a mission. The disciples know the long-awaited Messiah. The terror is the threshold to experiencing his sovereign love. Job, I think, in addition to feeling terror, profoundly felt God's love. *God showed up and spoke to him!* Children can perceive their parents' love in a moment of dressing down. We should expect, I think, that the love of the Lord of the universe will blow our hair back.

The terror moves quickly into a profound sense of God's mercy and person-specific love. It is like realizing that the being peering at me through the trees is looking at me because he loves me. He was watching me before I ever saw him. He has a right to eat me. But what motivates his gaze is love. It is both painful and good to be known by God. It's a feeling that binds you to him forever, with all of your being.

It is best expressed by Mr. Beaver, speaking of the Lion King, Aslan, in *The Lion, the Witch, and the Wardrobe*, by C. S. Lewis. Lucy has asked, on hearing Aslan described: "Is he quite safe?" Mr. Beaver snorts, "Safe! Of course he isn't safe. But he's good! He's the king, I tell you!"

You have been asking the question *Can I know God?* I have been striving to answer it in the affirmative. What I say now is not meant to belittle the effort, but to put it in its proper, life-changing perspective. The ultimate question is not *Do or can I know God?* It is *Does he know me?*

It is right to ask the questions. But expect to find that you are the one who needs to answer someone else's questions—someone who has the right and power and reality to be answered. Expect that in seeking to know God, you are no longer the one in pursuit. You are the pursued.

But don't run. Seated on the back of a loving lion, as Lucy found, is the best of all possible places to be.

For Further Thought and Discussion

Describe your experience. Can you think of an experience in which your coming to know has proven to be a coming to be known? Describe how it made you feel.

Consider knowing God. Have you had an experience of knowing God that was like this? If you haven't, is the prospect of being known by God the thing that you fear? What questions do you think he might ask you? Does this chapter offer any comfort?

Respond to the book. Having read this book, do you think that it successfully makes the case that knowing God is an ordinary act of knowing such as knowing your auto mechanic? Does it make the case that knowing happens? What are the strengths of the argument? How can the argument be improved?

Notes

Foreword

10   ...*and The Tacit Dimension.* Other works of Polanyi's that are favorites of mine are "Knowing and Being," and "The Logic of Tacit Inference," in Marjorie Grene, ed. *Knowing and Being: Essays by Michael Polanyi* (Chicago: University of Chicago Press, 1969), pp. 123–37, 138–58; "The Creative Imagination," in *Chemical and Engineering News* 44 (25 April 1966): 85–93; and "Science and Reality," in *British Journal for the Philosophy of Science* 18 (1967): 177–96. A fine biography of Polanyi is available on audio cassette: *Tacit Knowing, Truthful Knowing: The Life and Thought of Michael Polanyi,* Mars Hill Audio (Charlottesville, VA: Berea Publications, 1999). Marjorie Grene's *The Knower and the Known* (Berkeley: University of California Press, 1974) is a magnificent analysis of Western philosophy from a Polanyian perspective. My other work on Polanyi includes: *Contact With Reality: An Examination of Realism in the Work of Michael Polanyi* (Ph.D. Dissertation, Temple University, 1983); "A Polanyian Interpretation of Calvin's *Sensus Divinitatis*," *Presbyterion* 23. 1 (Spring 1997): 8–24; " 'Recalled to Life': Contact With Reality," *Tradition and Discovery* 26. 3: 72–83; "Learning to See: The Role of Authoritative Guides in Knowing," paper delivered at the Polanyi Society, Toronto, November, 2002. *Tradition and Discovery* is the official journal of the Polanyi Society. Their website is http://www.mwsc.edu/~polanyi

Chapter 1

16   ...*on a reasoned argument.* Philosophers known as Reformed Epistemologists, in particular, Alvin Plantinga, have been concerned to show that religious belief is rational even in the absence of specific reasons or proofs. See for example Plantinga's "Reason and Belief in God," in *Faith and Rationality,* Plantinga and Nicholas Wolterstorff, eds. (Notre Dame and London: University of Notre Dame Press, 1983), pp. 16–93.

18   ...*call it emotional fusion.* Psychologist Murray Bowen developed family systems therapy and the related concepts of emotional fusion and self-differentiation. See his *Family Ther-*

apy in Clinical Practice (New York: J. Aronson, 1978). Emotional fusion refers to an unhealthy emotional connectedness between persons in a family system.

Chapter 2

20 *...philosopher Bertrand Russell's books. Our Knowledge of the External World* (Chicago: University of Chicago Press, 1914).

21 *...know anything at all.* Skepticism is "the denial that knowledge or even rational belief is possible, either about some specific subject-matter ... or in any area whatsoever." (Simon Blackburn, *Oxford Dictionary of Philosophy* (Oxford: University Press, 1994)). See also Louis Pojman, *What Can We Know? An Introduction to the Theory of Knowledge* (Belmont, Ca.: Wadsworth, 1995), p. 9, and chs. 2, 3.

21 *...from modernism to postmodernism.* While this shift and its terminology has unfolded in connection with discussions of literature and interpretation, with a view to cultural developments, modernism and postmodernism have obvious epistemological implications. So, for example, Alistair McGrath, in *A Passion for Truth* (Downers Grove, Ill.: InterVarsity Press, 1996), identifies *modernism* with "the Enlightenment project," "a sustained effort on the part of its thinkers to develop objective science, universal morality and law, and autonomous art according to their inner logic," a belief in the "omnicompetence of human reason" (pp. 165, 163). A term developed by Francois Lyotard in 1979, *postmodernism* is defined by McGrath as a collapse of this confidence in reason, or in Lyotard's terse words, "an incredulity toward metanarratives," where a metanarrative is a grand, overarching explanation of the way things are. I tend to lump the cultural into the philosophical. Philosophers thus closely linked to modernism include all the philosophers of the Modern period, beginning with René Descartes, John Locke, David Hume, and Immanual Kant. Philosophers whose work has been closely linked to postmodernism include Friedrich Nietzsche, Jacques Derrida, Michel Foucault, and Richard Rorty. One thorough analysis of this shift to postmodernism is Roger Lundin's *The Culture of Interpretation: Christian Faith and the Postmodern World* (Grand Rapids: Eerdmans, 1993). It should also be noted that modernism holds no corner on the philosophical market of commitment to reason and objective truth. Modernism only put its own special signature on the dominating stream of Western philosophy since before Plato. Thus, in rejecting the ascendancy of reason, postmodernism opposes not just modernism but all of the Western tradition.

22 *...that this is nonsense.* Borrowing David Wells's title (Grand Rapids: Eerdmans, 1993), "no place for truth," this group includes philosophers (religion is emotion, not knowledge), pietists (religion is heart, not head), pluralists (all religions are true, so truth doesn't matter), postmodernists (there is no "true"), and plain ol' hypocrites (whose behavior doesn't embody their truth claims).

22 *...only Son, our Lord....* You can find this in the hymnbooks of most Christian churches.

24 *...define it, I can't. The Confessions of St. Augustine,* John K. Ryan, trans. (Garden City, N.Y.: Doubleday/Image Books, 1960), book 11, ch. 14.

Chapter 3

26 *...is infallible or certain.* People don't all use the term "certain" in exactly the same way. My argument in this chapter defines certainty as statements that can't turn out to be false, or that can't justifiably be doubted. What philosophers and all of us have been wishing for, I think it's reasonable to say, are statements anchored in such a way that they can't

turn out to be false. Whether or not we disagree as to terminology, the point of this chapter is that we have been motivated to attain an ideal that is false and misguided, and that in pursuit of it, we have made some assumptions about knowing that blind us in an unfortunate way to what actually occurs. To say the ideal is unattainable (hence skepticism) still assumes the ideal. We need to revise the ideal. The result, you will see, is far from skepticism, and it restores confidence and hope to us in our epistemic efforts. See Lesslie Newbigin, *Proper Confidence: Faith, Doubt and Certainty in Christian Discipleship* (Grand Rapids: Eerdmans, 1995), chs. 2, 3. See also the now very common rejection of foundationalism (the idea that there exist at least some statements which can't turn out to be false, from which the rest of our legitimate truth claims must be derivable), nicely summarized in Nicholas Wolterstorff's *Reason Within the Bounds of Religion* (Grand Rapids: Eerdmans, 1976).

I surmise that this misguided ideal of certainty has been invoked more rigorously in some contexts rather than others. Religion, Christianity in particular, has for centuries drawn pointed modernist attack. Take, for example, W. K. Clifford's famous aphorism, "It is wrong always, everywhere, and for anyone, to believe anything upon insufficient evidence" (*Lectures and Essays* [London: Macmillan and Co., 1886], quoted in Plantinga's "Reason and Belief in God," p. 24). Clifford was targeting religious belief as illicit. While Christian philosophers such as Alvin Plantinga have noted the self-referential inconsistency of Clifford's maxim, it nevertheless remains emblazoned, for example, with no additional justification, on the pre-preface page of the textbook I use to teach logic (Patrick Hurley, *A Concise Introduction to Logic,* 8th ed. [Belmont, CA: Wadsworth, 2000]). The misguided ideal continues to have unquestioning supporters.

What is more, I believe that Christian thinkers themselves embraced the ideal of certainty and attempted to massage their approach to meet its demands (Stephen R. Spencer, " 'Evangelical Modernists'? Evangelical Responses to Postmodernism and Postliberalism" [unpublished paper, 1999]). And finally, people considering Christianity, as well as believers even of long standing, may be more swayed by the ideal with respect to their beliefs than, say, scientists in pursuit of a discovery or people reading the newspaper.

27 ...*history of Western philosophy.* Far better introductions to the history of philosophy include the standard multivolume *History of Philosophy* by Frederick Copleston, S.J. (New York: Doubleday/Image, 1977), and two very readable one-volume introductions: Jostein Gaarder, *Sophie's World: A Novel About the History of Philosophy,* Paulette Moller, trans. (NewYork: Farrar, Strauss and Giroux, 1994); and Bryan Magee, *The Great Philosophers: An Introduction to Western Philosophy* (New York: Oxford University Press, 1987). Marjorie Grene's *The Knower and the Known* is her analysis of the key figures in the history of philosophy. All the major philosophers I talk about in this chapter are more fully described and evaluated in these works.

27 ...*has been to skepticism.* Further proof of this requires only that we check a few introductory texts in epistemology, such as Pojman's *What Can We Know,* and Paul K. Moser, Dwayne H. Mulder, and J. D. Trout, *The Theory of Knowledge: A Thematic Introduction* (New York: Oxford University Press, 1998), which begin and end with attention to skepticism and call it a corrective in our epistemic enterprise. Compare also *Epistemology: A Contemporary Introduction to the Theory of Knowledge* (New York: Routledge, 1998), in which author Robert Audi feels compelled at the outset to explain why he is *not* embedding his analysis in skepticism.

28 ...*faced a skeptical milieu.* Plato's most famous works are his *Republic,* which includes the Allegory of the Cave, and his other *Dialogues.*

28 ...*the object in question.* Aristotle's works include his *Categories,* the *Physics,* and the *Metaphysics.* He developed formal logic, as well as botanical classification. The medieval Roman

Catholic theologian Thomas Aquinas referred to Aristotle as "The Philosopher," and relied heavily on his insights where he took them to be consistent with Scripture.

30   ...*writing in the mid-1600s.* His philosophical works include *Meditations on First Philoso-phy,* and *Discourse on Method.* In addition, Descartes was a famous mathematician (Carte-sian coordinates, for example), and is also considered the father of psychology.

30   ...*philosopher, one of many.* Russell was also a mathematician, a British lord and politi-cian, and a social and religious critic. His prolific writings include: *Our Knowledge of the External World, Human Knowledge: Its Scope and Limits,* and *The Problems of Philosophy.*

31   ...*(Thank you, Friedrich Nietzsche.)* Nietzsche lived in the second half of the nineteenth century. His works include *The Twilight of the Idols, The Will to Power,* and *Thus Spake Zarathustra.* Nietzsche's work has recently gained in popularity as his thought has been recognized as a forerunner of postmodernism.

33   ...*just perceive our perceptions.* Marjorie Grene quips that Hume's is "a world with no non-sense, yet it is a world with no sense either, and that for one principal reason: that there is nobody in it" (*The Knower and the Known,* p. 102).

33   ...*justification would be foolproof.* The discussion begins with Plato's *Theatetus.* It is revived in the twentieth century by Roderick Chisholm in his *Theory of Knowledge* (Englewood Cliffs, NJ: Prentice-Hall, 1966), and followed by many attempts to specify what would count as a knowledge-determining account. In more recent years this effort known as "internalism" (insisting that for a claim to count as knowledge the knower recognize internally and give adequate justification for that claim) has been discarded by some in favor of "externalism" (the more modest claim that what is needed in order to have knowl-edge is not even this internal recognition or an airtight justification, but rather external conditions which when met count as grounds for the claim). Plantinga and many oth-ers have worked to develop externalism. See his *Warrant: The Current Debate* (New York: Oxford University Press, 1993), and *Warrant and Proper Function* (New York: Oxford University Press, 1993). Note how Platonic this search is, looking for a definition of the essence of knowledge, such that you can decide which instances make the cut and which don't.

34   ...*being restored to us.* Martin Heidegger and Maurice Merleau-Ponty, Continental philoso-phers in the early twentieth century, philosopher of language Ludwig Wittgenstein, and American pragmatist Richard Rorty are some thinkers whose rejection of modernism has led to new and fertile insights. In this respect their effort parallels that of Michael Polanyi.

Chapter 4

40   ...*minute and touch him.* Richard Winter, "Knowing the Invisible, Inaudible, Untouch-able God: Between the Garden, Galilee and Glory," in *Presbyterion* 25.2 (1999): 67–79.

Chapter 5

41   ...*a neatly deduced human system.* See Ronald Nash's *Worldviews in Conflict: Choosing Chris-tianity in a World of Ideas* (Grand Rapids: Zondervan, 1992), ch. 4. Nash speaks to "the large numbers of Christians who, regrettably, are irrationalists in their understanding and portrayal of the Christian faith. He offers a response to the claim of W. T. Stace, in a 1955 article, that "God is utterly and forever beyond the reach of the logical intellect

or of any intellectual comprehension…" This chapter of mine takes a different approach from Nash's in responding to the same misperception about knowledge of God.

42 …*replaces belief or faith.* Aquinas, for example, thought this (Copleston, vol. II, part 2, ch. 32).

42 …*"making room for faith." Critique of Pure Reason,* Norman Kemp Smith, trans. (New York: St. Martins, 1965), p. 29.

42 …*not-really-human knowledge.* Romanticism "was partly a reaction against the stiff rationality of the Enlightenment," says the entry in Blackburn's *Oxford Dictionary of Philosophy.*" Knowledge of the Absolute "cannot be acquired by rational and analytic means, but only by emotional and intuitive absorption within the process [of self realization in nature]."

42 …*surface in contemporary theology.* The Jesus Seminar, while not directly focused on this agenda, nevertheless assumed its legitimacy as it produced its own version of the Gospels. See *The Five Gospels: The Search for the Authentic Words of Jesus,* by Robert W. Funk, Roy W. Hoover, and The Jesus Seminar (New York: Macmillan, 1993); and a scholarly response, Michael J. Wilkins and J. P. Moreland, eds., *Jesus Under Fire* (Grand Rapids: Zondervan, 1995).

43 …*religion outside rational knowing.* Stanley Grenz and Roger Olson, in *Twentieth-Century Theology: God and the World in a Transitional Age* (Downers Grove, Ill.: InterVarsity Press, 1992), group recent centuries' theological trends under the headings, *transcendence* and *immanence.* Efforts such as the Jesus Seminar fall in the immanence category. Theologies that emphasize the otherness of religious experience fall in the category of transcendence.

43 …*thoughts than your thoughts.'"* Isaiah 55:8–9.

Chapter 6

46 …*Magic Eye 3-D pictures? Magic Eye: A New Way of Looking at the World,* by N. E. Thing Enterprises, Magic Eye Inc. (Kansas City: Andrews McMeel, 1993). This was the first of several such books. Also see the Magic Eye website (www.magic.com) for online samples.

Chapter 8

63 …*lies beneath the surface."* Patrick Hurley, *A Concise Introduction to Logic,* p. 569.

64 …*is to look for." Meno,* trans. W. K. C. Guthrie, in *Plato: The Collected Dialogues,* ed. Edith Hamilton and Huntington Cairns (Princeton: Princeton University Press, 1961), p. 363.

64 …*"just the facts, ma'am."* A phrase from the old television show, *Dragnet.*

Chapter 9

70 …*intrinsically* caring *and* coping. Martin Heidegger, *Being and Time,* trans. John MacQuarrie and Edward Robinson (New York: Harper and Row, 1962), ch. 6.

71 …*that will bless it.* Genesis 1:26–27; 2:15; Psalm 8.

71 …*just and righteous rule.* One of many such passages is 2 Samuel 23:3, 4.

Chapter 10

79 ...*pray, "Your kingdom come...."* Matthew 6:9.

79 ...*rouse a deaf world."* *The Problem of Pain* (New York: Macmillan, 1962), p. 93.

79 ...*the throne of God"* Hebrews 12:3.

Chapter 11

88 ...*says, as God's clothes.* John Calvin, *Institutes of the Christian Religion,* trans. Ford Lewis Battles, Library of Christian Classics 20 (Philadelphia: Westminster Press, 1960), book 1, ch. 5. 1.

Chapter 12

91 ...*bear on other things.* Maurice Merleau-Ponty explores this bodily perception in his *Phenomenology of Perception* (London: Routledge and Kegan Paul, 1962). See also Part 4 of Meek, *Contact with Reality.*

92 ...*ethos, Aristotle would say.* *Rhetoric,* in *The Basic Works of Aristotle,* ed. Richard McKeon (New York: Random House, 1941), book 1, ch. 1, book 2, ch. 1.

92 ...*less-healthy approaches to life.* Daniel Goleman, *Emotional Intelligence* (New York: Bantam Books, 1995). EQ bears a striking resemblance to the insights contained in the Bible's book of Proverbs, which stresses the good benefit of self control, diligence, hopeful response to setbacks, empathy, managing emotions in relationships, patience, peacemaking, thinking before acting, ability to resolve conflicts, awareness and management of one's own feelings, treating people with understanding and respect, and delayed gratification. Summing it up, Proverbs 4:23 says, "Above all else, guard your heart, for it is the wellspring of life." Proverbs 3:7–8 says that fearing the LORD and shunning evil "will bring health to your body and nourishment to your bones."

93 ...*and intentionally its cultivation.* Psychotherapist Eugene Gendlin came to recognize and now capitalize on the fact that the people who profit from psychotherapy are those who know how to listen to their own body sense (*Focusing* [New York: Bantam Books, 1981]). Our bodies, he says, can know things that conceptually we are keeping from ourselves. The method he develops, focusing, involves quieting oneself to pay attention to bodily feelings, then putting words on those feelings and holding our knee-jerk rationalizations in abeyance long enough to see if other words fit more aptly.

The process that Gendlin describes is, I believe, the central nerve of all acts of coming to know, all learnings. We are incurably verbal creatures, and that in itself is a good thing. But words like swords or chain saws work powerfully only as we keep them sharpened. I believe every time that we use a concept we are assessing the rightness of its fit to the situation, or at least we ought to be. All of us know that people can do this well or poorly. When we say that someone is glib or gives pat answers, we are saying that he or she is insensitive to the situation, blind to how the words do not fit. On the other hand, the book of Proverbs says that an aptly fitting word is "like apples of gold in settings of silver" (25:11). When we come into a learning situation, we have new concepts thrown at us that we need to grow into, to learn to feel from the inside. If we are artists, we are perhaps inventing fresh concepts that open people's eyes to what they have been feeling but hadn't yet put words on. In all of this, what is going on is a matching of words to our lived body feel of things. Gendlin's point, and my belief, is that we will be better knowers as we learn how to cultivate our lived sense of the real. But that requires a model of knowing that accredits it rather than denies it.

93   *...that will he reap."* Galatians 6:7.

Chapter 13

99   *...patients to think differently.* David Burns, M.D., *Feeling Good: The New Mood Therapy* (New York: Avon Books, 1980).

99   *...see, and the knowledgeable."* (New York: HarperPerennial, 1974), p. 20.

99   *...so critical to knowing?* I have explored this topic further in "Learning to See: The Role of Authoritative Guides in Knowing," paper for the Polanyi Society meetings, Toronto, Fall 2002.

103   *...every legitimate human act.* I am indebted to my colleague theologian Mike Williams for guiding me in this insight. A fitting match of method and subject!

104   *...but have eternal life."* John 3:16.

105   *...the benefits of it.* Again, Mike Williams's insights.

105   *...the desert to see?"* Matthew 11:7–10.

Chapter 14

109   *...the road to Emmaus.* Luke 24:13–35.

110   *...then enter his glory?"* "Messiah" is the NIV marginal reading for "Christ."

111   *...than Solomon is here."* Matthew 12:42.

111   *...Damascus to persecute them.* Acts 9:1–19.

112   *...am a sinful man!"* Luke 5:1–8.

112   *...Lord and my God!"* John 20:28.

Chapter 15

118   *...of our verbal claims.* Hurley lists these as criteria for testing hypotheses, *Concise Introduction to Logic*, p. 577–78. See also David L. Wolfe, *Epistemology: The Justification of Belief* (Downers Grove, Ill.: InterVarsity Press, 1982), ch. 3.

122   *...God's power and goodness.* 1 Timothy 6:16.

122   *...to be with me."* John 14:2–3.

122   *...lead you to repentance.* Romans 2:4.

122   *...will come, he says.* 2 Peter 3:10.

Chapter 16

128   *...are able to tell."* Contact With Reality, pp. 81–82.

128   *...imagining someone's destiny truly.* Caroline J. Simon, *The Disciplined Heart: Love, Destiny, and Imagination* (Grand Rapids: Eerdmans, 1997).

133   ...*saw a crocus yesterday."* Lewis, "The Grand Miracle," in *God In The Dock: Essays on Theology and Ethics*, ed. Walter Hooper (Grand Rapids: Eerdmans, 1970), p. 87.

133   ...*he burns as firewood!* Isaiah 44:6–20.

Chapter 17

137   ...*better term is confidence.* This is Lesslie Newbigin's main claim in *Proper Confidence.*

138   ...*of unlocking the real.* Newbigin says "I can only affirm the objectivity of a truth claim which I make by committing myself to live and act in accordance with this claim." *Proper Confidence*, p. 75.

138   ...*can contribute unique insights.* Dale Cannon, "Tacit Knowing as Knowing by Acquaintance, Rather than Knowing by Representation: Some Implications," paper for the Polanyi Society Conference, Loyola University, Chicago, June 8–10, 2001, p. 12.

139   ...*grand drama of redemption.* My colleague, theologian Mike Williams, and others. See Michael S. Horton, *Covenant and Eschatology: The Divine Drama* (Louisville: Westminster John Knox, 2002), pp. 9–12.

139   ...*in store for us.* Hebrews 1. Hear also songwriter Michael Card's piece, "The Final Word," included in *The Life* (Chatsworth, CA: Sparrow, 1988).

140   ...*speak on my own."* John 7:17.

Chapter 18

145   ...*themselves and to others.* Here I have in mind specifically Christians who maintain a commitment to the objective authority of the Bible. However, I think a case could be made that for those who have rejected this commitment, that they too have maintained a modern model of knowledge, but have concluded instead that the Bible falls short of that model. The thrust of the work of Newbigin and others such as W. Stephen Gunter (*Resurrection Knowledge: Recovering the Gospel for a Postmodern Church* [Nashville: Abingdon Press, 1999]) indicates their belief that espousing this alternative, Polanyian, model of knowing offers a fresh direction and one that turns out to be more biblically compatible.

Chapter 19

150   ...*who searches for it."* Proverbs 11:27.

150   ...*the obstinacy of belief.* "On Obstinacy in Belief," in *The World's Last Night and Other Essays* (New York: Harcourt Brace Jovanovitch, 1973), pp. 13–30.

150   ...*simply will not do.* Lewis, *Mere Christianity* (New York: MacMillan, 1943), pp. 55–56.

152   ...*their rest in Thee."* *Confessions*, bk. 1, ch. 1. See also C. S. Lewis, *Surprised by Joy: The Shape of My Early Life* (London: G. Bles, 1955), and John Eldredge, *The Journey of Desire: Searching for the Life We've Only Dreamed Of* (Nashville: Thomas Nelson, 2000). My own personal "surprised by joy" experience involved reading Newbigin's *Proper Confidence* twenty-five years after finishing my dissertation on Polanyi's realism. In one sentence, Newbigin suggested that reality has that telltale feature of intimating things we may yet discover just because it is the work of God, the ultimate Person, for whom we long. In one blinding moment of joy, I saw that what had tantalized me about my topic was pro-

foundly linked to God, and I understood why it had drawn me so powerfully. It made sense of my life work.

Chapter 20

156 ...was depleted of oxygen. Grene's example, *The Knower and the Known*, p. 73.

157 ...human beings are prone. This work is referenced fully in chapter 13.

162 ...reading of old books." "On the Reading of Old Books," in *God in the Dock*, p. 202.

164 ...other gods before me." Exodus 20:3.

164 ...beings are incurably religious. *Institutes*, book 1, ch.3. 1.

164 ...did not recognize him." John 1: 3–5, 10.

Chapter 21

168 ... Son, whom I love..." Luke 3:21–23.

168 ... fulfilled in your hearing." Luke 4:16–21.

168 ... we expect someone else?" Luke 7:18–23.

174 ... who diligently seek him. Hebrews 11:6.

Chapter 22

175 ...which were profoundly rewarded. *Pilgrim at Tinker Creek*, ch. 11: "Stalking."

177 ...or covenant, a marriage. Mike Williams and I have developed this concept that we are calling covenant epistemology. Others who have utilized the term independently and for somewhat different purposes include Steve Garber, educational consultant to universities, and Michael Horton, in *Covenant and Eschatology*. See also Parker Palmer's insights concerning "truth as troth" (*To Know as We Are Known: Education as a Spiritual Journey* [San Francisco: Harper SanFrancisco, 1993], ch. 4).

179 ...person further into truth. John 7:17; Psalm 25:14.

Chapter 23

184 ...to believe the truth. (New York: Macmillan, 1956), chs. 7, 13.

185 ...knowing" if you like. Lesslie Newbigin's wonderful description, *Proper Confidence*, p. 67.

186 ...We "love his appearing." These last three biblical claims are loose renderings of 1 Corinthians 13:12, 1 Peter 1:8, 2 Timothy 4:8.

186 ...would know Christ better. Ephesians 1:15–17 offers a good example of an apostle's prayer for believers' knowledge of Christ.

187 ...him for that day." 2 Timothy 1:12, italics mine.

187 ...were made: 'Follow me.'" *Proper Confidence*, p. 105.

Chapter 25

193   ...*I was found of thee.* Anonymous hymn, 1878. *Trinity Hymnal* (Philadelphia: Great Commission, 1990).

194   ...*and named him Samson.* Judges 13.

194   ...*King, the* LORD *Almighty."* Isaiah 6:5.

194   ...*in dust and ashes.* Job 38–42.

195   ...*am a sinful man!"* Luke 5:1–11.

195   ...*it was completely calm."* Matthew 8:23–27.

195   ...*and am no more."* Psalm 39:13.

196   ...*has been at work.* See Isaiah 28:23-29, where the prophet says that Yahweh is the one who teaches the farmer to farm.

196   ...*king, I tell you!" The Lion, the Witch, and the Wardrobe* (New York: Macmillan, 1956), ch. 8.